RONALD
REAGAN

RONALD REAGAN

George Sullivan

REVISED EDITION

JULIAN MESSNER

Published by Julian Messner,
a division of Silver Burdett Press, Inc., Simon & Schuster, Inc.
Prentice Hall Bldg., Englewood Cliffs, NJ 07632
JULIAN MESSNER and colophon are
trademarks of Simon & Schuster, Inc.

Manufactured in the United States of America

10 9 8 7 6 5 4 3 2 1

Library of Congress Cataloging-in-Publication Data

Sullivan, George.
    Ronald Reagan/George Sullivan.—Rev. ed.
        p.   cm.
    Summary: Traces the life of the fortieth president including his
childhood, film career, and his years in state and national politics.
    1. Reagan, Ronald—Juvenile literature.   2. Presidents—United
States—Biography—Juvenile literature.   [1. Reagan,
Ronald.   2. Presidents.]   I. Title.
E877.S85   1991
973.927'092—dc20
[B]   91-3744
                                                                  CIP
                                                                   AC

ISBN 0-671-74537-9

Contents

I

New Beginning

On Sunday, January 20, 1985, in a quiet private ceremony in the White House, Ronald Wilson Reagan took the constitutional oath to begin his second term as the fortieth president of the United States.

With his left hand on an open Bible held by his wife, Nancy, and his right hand raised, the president repeated the words of the chief justice of the United States, pledging to "preserve, protect and defend the Constitution."

In November 1984, Reagan had defeated Walter F. Mondale in an electoral landslide. To go with his 525 electoral votes, the biggest total in the history of presidential politics, Reagan had piled up a mighty popular vote.

Indeed, as Reagan got set to begin his second term, he ranked as one of the most popular political figures of twentieth-century America.

There was much else that was remarkable about Ronald Reagan. He was the oldest man ever to serve as President. Two weeks after taking the inaugural oath in 1985, Reagan celebrated his seventy-fourth birthday.

To get an idea of how extraordinary that fact is, consider

that George Washington and Thomas Jefferson were fifty-seven years old when first inaugurated; Abraham Lincoln, fifty-two; Franklin D. Roosevelt, fifty-one (Roosevelt, after being elected four times, was only sixty-three when he died); Dwight Eisenhower, sixty-two; and John F. Kennedy, forty-three.

Reagan was born in 1911, only eight years after the Wright brothers' first successful flight of a motor-powered plane at Kitty Hawk, North Carolina. The horse and wagon was still the chief means of transportation. The first commercial radio station did not begin broadcasting until 1920. Television, of course, came much later.

At seventy-four, Reagan seemed younger than his years, thanks to a vigorous and athletic appearance. His face was rosy. He had more wrinkles in his face than he did four years earlier, at the beginning of his first presidential term, but not many. All in all, he was in remarkable physical condition.

Reagan was brought up in a series of small towns in Illinois, with a brief stay in Chicago. He often expressed the values that prevailed when and where he grew up. During his youth, he learned that "energy and hard work are the only ingredients needed for success." At home and at school he learned "the great ideals of our nation." Morality and religion were woven into the fabric of his life.

After graduating from high school, Reagan went off to Eureka College in Eureka, Illinois. There he concentrated on sports, politics, and acting.

Twenty-four of the forty American presidents were admitted to the bar as attorneys. Others were farmers or soldiers. Reagan was unique. Acting was his profession. After college, he was a sports announcer for a Midwest radio station; then he became a movie actor and appeared in fifty-three films. From the movies, Reagan went into television. It was no accident that he became exceptional as a public speaker and TV performer.

Reagan became active in union affairs and politics in Hollywood. In 1964, he made a stirring nationally televised speech on behalf of Barry Goldwater, the Republican candidate for president. In the speech, Reagan attacked high taxes, wasteful government, and soaring welfare costs.

The speech did more good for Reagan's political career than it did for Barry Goldwater's. Two years later, in 1966, Reagan won his first political office when he was elected governor of California.

Reagan campaigned unsuccessfully for the Republican presidential nomination in 1968 and again in 1976. He tried again in 1980 and won. That fall he defeated Democratic incumbent Jimmy Carter to win his first presidential term.

Reagan was effective in his first term as president, able to get things done. With his charm and apparent sincerity, his openness and optimism, he was a natural leader.

Reagan was also effective because he was—as he was sometimes called—the Great Communicator. Out of his experience as a motion picture, radio, and television performer, Reagan had learned how to use his voice and be persuasive. He was a salesman.

But like every good salesman, Reagan believed in his product. He believed in the traditional values of hard work, self-reliance, family ties, and patriotism.

When he took over the presidency in 1981, Reagan had a definite program, and he set certain goals for his administration. One goal was to build up the military. Reagan would seek to strengthen the military systems of both the United States and its European allies. Another goal was to get tough with the Soviet Union. Reagan believed that the Soviet Union was an "evil empire." That nation's aggressiveness must be opposed, said Reagan, by expansion of the armed might of the United States. "Peace through strength" would be Reagan's policy.

The reduction of taxes was an aim of Reagan's domestic policy. In his first year in office, Reagan would push through the biggest income tax cut in U.S. history. In addition, Reagan promised to get the government "off the backs" of the American people. This meant embarking on a program of deregulation that would wipe out many government rules and restrictions.

Reagan was one of the few presidents to offer a definite program, and he achieved most of it. In pursuit of his goals, he changed not only America but the world.

2

A "Tom Sawyer Boyhood"

We were poor, but we didn't know we were poor." On a number of occasions, that's how Ronald Reagan has described his boyhood. Although his family was never prosperous, Reagan's memories of growing up were mostly happy ones.

Reagan was the second son of John "Jack" Edward Reagan and Nelle Wilson Reagan. He was born on February 6, 1911, in the front bedroom of the family's five-room apartment above the store where his father worked in Tampico, Illinois. He was christened Ronald Wilson Reagan.

His father was a handsome and muscular Irish-American who sold shoes for a living, often as a department-store shoe clerk. He was a restless, ambitious man whose dream was to own a big and fancy shoe emporium that would make him rich.

But Mr. Reagan's dreams were often sidetracked by a weakness he had. Sometimes he drank too much. As a boy growing up, Ronald was aware of this. From the sharp odor of whiskey on his father's breath, his occasional absences from home, or the loud arguments at night, Ronald knew of his father's struggle with alcoholism.

One winter evening, when Ronald was eleven, he came home to find his father stretched out on the front porch in a drunken stupor, his hair soaked by melting snow. Ronald dragged his father into the house and managed to get him to bed. Within a few days, the incident was forgotten, and Mr. Reagan was his proud and vigorous self once more.

Ronald's mother, a lean, strong woman of Scotch-Irish descent, explained to her two young sons that alcoholism was a sickness. She said that they should help their father and love him.

Reagan developed a deep dislike for hard drinking out of this experience. As an adult, he would limit his own drinking to an occasional glass or two of wine with dinner.

Although there was only two years' difference in their ages, Ronald was very different from Neil, his older brother. Neil, who became a Los Angeles advertising executive, was called Moon by his parents, a nickname taken from the popular comic strip "Moon Mullins." Ronald was nicknamed Dutch. He got the name from his father, who thought that he looked like a "fat little Dutchman" at birth.

Moon, like his father, was big and boisterous. He was raised as a Catholic, which was his father's faith.

Dutch was the smaller and quieter of the two boys. His mother raised him as a Protestant, a member of the Christian church.

Both parents encouraged the two boys to judge people as individuals, not by their religion, race, or color. When the early film classic *The Birth of a Nation* was being shown in their hometown, Moon and Dutch were not allowed to see it, although their friends flocked to the theater where it was being shown. "It deals with the Ku Klux Klan against the

A 1913 photo of the Reagan family. From left: "Jack" Reagan, sons, Neil and Ronald, and Nellie Wilson Reagan.

colored folks," Mr. Reagan declared, "and I'll be damned if anyone in this family will go see it."

Another time, Mr. Reagan was on the road as a shoe salesman, and checked into a small-town hotel. The room clerk told him he would like the hotel because it didn't accept Jews. Mr. Reagan became furious. He told the clerk that he was a Catholic and that the hotel would probably soon be turning away Catholics, too. He picked up his suitcase, stormed out of the hotel, and ended up spending the night in his car.

In her quiet way, Mrs. Reagan dominated the home. She saw to it that the family attended lectures and plays. She wanted both of her sons to be well-educated. She worked hard to teach Dutch how to read before he went to school, sitting with him at night and reading books to him while following each word with her finger.

One evening, young Dutch was lying on the floor with a newspaper. "What are you doing?" his father asked.

Reagan and his third grade classmates in Tampico, Illinois. He is in the second row, first boy on left.

"Reading," Dutch answered.

"Well, read something," said Mr. Reagan.

And Dutch did. His mother was so proud that she called in the neighbors to hear her son read aloud.

During the first years of Moon's and Dutch's life, the family lived in several small towns in western Illinois. The frequent moves were made necessary by Mr. Reagan's search for work. Mr. Reagan had a job at the Fair Store. Galesburg was next, then Monmouth, and then back to Tampico.

When Dutch was nine, the family settled in Dixon, Illinois—population 15,700—some ninety miles west of Chicago. There the Reagans put down roots. "All of us have a place to go back to," says Reagan in his autobiography. "Dixon is that place for me."

The Reagan family rented a two-story frame house at the top of a hill on Hennepin Avenue. Today, the house is open to the public, and tens of thousands of tourists visit it each year.

Reagan has called his Dixon years a "Tom Sawyer boyhood." During summer vacations, he and his brother fished, swam, and rowed canoes on the Rock River, which flowed through the center of town. They raised rabbits and collected birds' eggs. In winter, they skated or coasted on their Flexible Flyer sled all the way down Peoria Avenue to the river.

Among their friends were the O'Malley boys, George and Edward, with whom they played football in the side yard. Sometimes, in the summer, they slept on the O'Malleys' screened-in porch.

In Dixon, Dutch finished elementary school and went on to high school. There he played football and basketball and took part in track and swimming meets.

Football was his favorite sport. In other sports, he was handicapped by poor eyesight. In baseball, for example,

12 years old.

when he stood at the plate, he was unable to see the ball until it was about two feet in front of him. He scarcely had time to get the bat off his shoulder, much less lash out a hit.

But in football his poor eyesight was not a great problem. He could make out the ball carrier clearly enough to get his arms around him and bring him down.

Dutch was not aware he was nearsighted. He thought everyone saw distant objects indistinctly.

Then one day the family was out for a ride in the country. Moon was reading highway signs that Dutch could hardly see. Dutch borrowed his mother's glasses, and when he put them on, the highway signs came into sharp focus.

Not long after, his mother had Dutch fitted with black-rimmed glasses. Although the glasses solved his vision problem, Dutch hated wearing them. (This was a time before contact lenses; horn-rimmed spectacles were all that were available to correct conditions like nearsightedness.)

When it came to playing football, Dutch's poor vision was not nearly as much of a liability as his size—or lack of it. As a high-school freshman, he stood only five-foot-three and weighed 108 pounds. The school did not have a uniform small enough to fit him.

But during his senior year, Dutch shot up to nearly six feet. He weighed 165 pounds. He became the team's right guard in the starting lineup.

Dutch was a powerful swimmer. During the summers, he worked as a lifeguard at Lowell Park, a recreation area on the Rock River near Dixon. He is said to have put a notch in a log every time he saved a person from drowning. In seven summers as a lifeguard, he made seventy-seven notches.

Dutch joined the drama society and appeared in class plays at Dixon High School. An English teacher named B. J. Frazer, a slim, quiet man, taught drama. From him, Dutch learned basic acting skills. Frazer made his students "think" the roles they played instead of walking through them mechanically.

In 1928, the year that Dutch graduated from high school, attending college was much more the exception than the rule. It was simply too expensive for most families of the day. And many people considered college a waste of time. They thought it was far better for a young man or woman to spend those four years at a job, earning money.

That's the way Dutch's brother felt. After graduating from Dixon High, Moon had gotten a job at a local cement plant.

But Dutch had different ideas. In high school, he had been an achiever. He had been president of the student body and the drama club. He had been vice-president of the Hi-Y, an organization dedicated to promoting "clean speech, clean sports, clean living, and clean scholarship." In addition, his high-school marks were good. Though not exceptional, they were good enough to allow him to play sports. And in those days, a high-school diploma was all that was needed to gain admission to college. With a high-school career like that, college was the logical step.

Not only did Dutch plan to go to college, he had made up his mind about what college he wanted to attend. An idol of Dutch's, a Dixon football hero named Garland Waggoner, had gone to Eureka College in Eureka, Illinois. Dutch wanted to follow in his footsteps.

There was another incentive. The girl that Dutch had been dating, Margaret "Mugs" Cleaver, would also be entering Eureka. She was the daughter of the minister to the First Christian Church in Dixon. Dutch and Mugs had played the romantic leads in the class production of Philip Barry's *You and I.*

Mugs's father, the Reverend Ben Cleaver, encouraged Dutch to apply. Although he had never seen Eureka College, there was no doubt in Dutch's mind that that was where he would go.

3

Eureka

Toward the end of his presidential campaign in 1980, Ronald Reagan visited Eureka College and spoke at a pep rally. He said, "As far as I am concerned, everything good that has happened to me—everything—started here on this campus in those four years that are such a part of my life."

Reagan was not exaggerating. It was during his student days at Eureka that Reagan first demonstrated his skills as a public speaker, as someone who could address a crowd and influence it toward achieving a particular goal. It was at Eureka that Reagan first became seriously involved in politics and acting, the careers that he would pursue throughout his adult life.

Reagan first arrived at Eureka in the fall of 1928. (*Eureka* is a Greek word that means "I have found it." *Eureka* is also the motto of California, the state that Reagan would one day govern.) With its five main red-brick buildings, its rolling lawns and stately elms, Eureka College was a quiet and comfortable place. There were 250 students at the college that year, 130 boys and 120 girls.

At the edge of the city of Eureka in central Illinois, about twenty miles from Peoria, Eureka was the first college in Illinois and the third in the nation to admit women on an equal basis with men.

Dutch arrived at Eureka with a big steamer trunk containing his belongings and $400 that he had saved from his summers working as a lifeguard.

Not long after his arrival, he was able to convince the school scholarship office of his prowess in swimming and football. The school reduced his tuition by half, from $180 to $90 a year, and provided him with a job to pay his board. The job was washing dishes at a fraternity house.

Dutch became involved in a wide range of campus activities. He became a reporter for the school paper, *The Pegasus,* and a member of the school debate team.

Thanks to a boyfriend of one of Mugs's sisters, Dutch was accepted by Tau Kappa Epsilon, one of the several national fraternities on the Eureka campus.

Mugs pledged the Delta Theta sorority. When they weren't attending classes, she and Dutch were almost always together. They went to weekly dances at Dutch's fraternity house and to church together every Sunday.

Dutch tried out for the football team. "He was a plugger," Ralph McKinzie, the Eureka coach, once recalled. "He was not a star, but he was very conscientious and dedicated and worked very hard." McKinzie admired Dutch's skills as a blocker and tackler and made him the team's starting guard halfway through his sophomore season.

It was as a broadcaster, not as a gridiron star, that McKinzie best remembers Dutch: "I can remember after practice, he'd pull out a broom handle or something and pretend it was a microphone and start broadcasting games— names, players, everything. Just as real as it could be. The kids would all stop dressing just to listen to him."

The biggest excitement of Dutch's freshman year at Eureka was the school's financial crisis. Reagan has described Eureka as a school that was "perpetually broke." In 1928, the school hit a financial low point, hovering on the brink of bankruptcy.

Bert Wilson, the school's new president, proposed a money-saving plan that was based on dropping some courses and letting go the faculty members who had been teaching them.

Although the plan might have solved the school's financial crisis, it would have eliminated courses that some juniors and seniors needed to graduate. The plan was to be announced to the students when they returned from Thanksgiving vacation.

But the students learned of the plan before the announcement was made. Opposition to it developed quickly. Students and faculty members discussed going out on strike unless the courses were kept.

Dutch was the freshman representative on the strike committee. Chosen to address the student body, he won their support with an emotion-charged speech that got the students and faculty on their feet and cheering.

The strike was called and it succeeded. Within a week, President Wilson had resigned. No classes were dropped. No faculty members were dismissed.

Reagan's first brush with politics had been an unqualified triumph. The incident made a deep impression upon him. "I discovered that night," he would write in his autobiography, "that an audience has a feel to it and, in the parlance of the theater, that audience and I were together."

After Dutch had completed his freshman year at Eureka, he learned from his mother that Moon was fed up with working at the cement plant and wanted to go to college—to Eureka. Dutch got his older brother a campus job and, because Moon had played high-school football, a partial scholarship. His brother joined Dutch at Eureka in the fall of 1929.

Dutch displayed his theatrical skill as a member of

Eureka's drama society. He appeared in fourteen plays. In his junior year, he played the role of a Greek shepherd who is strangled to death in Edna St. Vincent Millay's *Aria da Capo*. Mugs Cleaver was also featured.

The Eureka drama department entered the play in the annual Eva Le Gallienne competition at Northwestern University, which attracted top schools from the East and Midwest. The Eureka offering finished a surprising third in the competition, and Dutch received an honorable-mention citation for his performance.

Dutch earned letters in football, swimming, and track at Eureka. He was the college's leading swimmer, and the swim team's coach during his junior and senior years.

Dutch served two years on the student senate, becoming president as a senior. He worked on the yearbook staff for two years, was president of the boosters club, was a cheerleader for the basketball team, and also held a job in the dining room throughout his four college years.

Studies? Classes? Little has been said or written concern-

Dutch Reagan with fellow members of the Eureka College Student Senate.

ing the academic side of Dutch's college career. It is known, however, that he had an exceptional memory, one that was almost photographic in the way it could retain information.

The night before an exam, Dutch would take the course textbook and flip through it for an hour or so. The next day, he would breeze through the exam.

Dutch graduated from Eureka in 1932 with a bachelor of arts degree in social science and economics. But graduation did not end Reagan's relationship with Eureka.

He made his first return to the campus in 1941, after he had begun his career in motion pictures. He was on hand for the one hundredth anniversary of the college in 1955. Two years later, he delivered the commencement address on the twenty-fifth anniversary of his graduation, and he was awarded the honorary degree of doctor of humane letters.

He and his brother attended the formal opening of the Reagan Physical Education Center in 1970, and in 1982, as president, he delivered a major foreign-policy address at graduation exercises on the fiftieth anniversary of his own graduation.

In 1984, not long after his seventy-third birthday, Reagan returned to the campus yet another time, underscoring again the deep affection for Eureka that continued throughout his life.

4

1932

Early in January 1981, several weeks after he had defeated Jimmy Carter but before he had been inaugurated for his first term as president, *Time* magazine named Ronald Reagan "Man of the Year." He was chosen not simply because he had risen so "smoothly and gracefully" to the presidency, but also because of the high hopes he represented for the future.

In interviewing the president-elect, an editor of *Time* asked him to pinpoint the year that was most important to him in forming his views. Reagan thought for a while, then answered, "Nineteen thirty-two."

Nineteen thirty-two. That was the year that Dutch Reagan turned twenty-one, graduated from Eureka, and went home to Dixon to serve as a lifeguard for the summer.

It was a year the nation was gripped by the Great Depression. More than 12 million workers were jobless. The most popular song of the day was "Brother, Can You Spare a Dime?"

Some 20,000 veterans of the World War (it had not yet been given the Roman numeral I) marched on Washington to demand bonus money for their military service. The marchers were routed by troops under the command of General Douglas MacArthur. The story was big news in Dixon, where the destitute lined up for bread and coffee at Newman's Garage.

In the spring of 1932, the cement plant where Neil Reagan had worked closed down, putting a thousand local residents out of work. The Fashion Boot Store, where Dutch's father had been a partner, closed, too. Mr. Reagan then worked at a series of odd jobs, but most of the family's income was provided by Mrs. Reagan, who took a job as a seamstress.

The Reagans were forced to rent out rooms in their apartment to boost their income. The family lived in one room and cooked on a hotplate.

As summer drew to an end, Dutch knew that he would have to find a full-time job. But prospects were bleak.

He heard of a sales job in the sporting goods section of Montgomery Ward and applied for it. It paid $12.50 for six days and two or three nights of work a week. But Dutch lost out to another Eureka graduate.

One day, B. J. Frazer, his former high-school drama teacher, talked to Dutch. He told him he should think about a career in communications, the field in which he had displayed so much talent.

In those pretelevision days, communications meant radio, which was fast becoming a major source of family entertainment. Every night families throughout America gathered in their living rooms to listen to comedy programs, adventure dramas, and music. Children hurried home from school to hear such adventure shows as "Superman" and "Jack Armstrong, All-American Boy."

The movies, like radio, were mushrooming in popularity in 1932. The Dixon theater offered such films as *Winner Take All*, with James Cagney; *Horse Feathers*, with the Marx Brothers; and *Red-Headed Woman*, with Jean Harlow. The biggest hit of the year was *Grand Hotel,* which starred Greta Garbo, John Barrymore, Joan Crawford, Wallace Beery, and Lionel Barrymore.

Chicago was the regional radio center for the Midwest. Dutch hitchhiked there to make the rounds of the stations. He soon found that scores of other young men were looking for jobs, too. Because of his lack of experience, no one was interested in hiring him.

But at the NBC studios in Chicago, a young woman told Dutch that it was a mistake for him to be job-hunting in Chicago. "Go out in what we call the sticks," she said, "and try some of the smaller stations."

Dutch took the woman's advice. Not long after, he presented himself at the studios of station WOC in Davenport, Iowa, which is about seventy miles west of Dixon on the Iowa-Illinois border.

Peter MacArthur, the station manager, told Dutch that WOC had been advertising for a new announcer for a month and had just made a choice. Dutch's heart sank. Angry at himself for not having known of the opening, Dutch blurted out, "How in the hell does a guy ever get to be a sports announcer if he can't get inside a station?"

Impressed by Dutch's spirit, MacArthur agreed to give him a tryout. He sat Dutch in a studio before a microphone and told him, "When the red light goes on, tell me about a football game, and make me see it."

Reagan described a game he had played in for Eureka, beginning, "Here we are going into the fourth quarter on a cold November afternoon, the long, blue shadows settling over the field, the wind whipping in through the empty end of the stadium."

MacArthur loved it. He offered Dutch $5 and round-trip bus fare from Dixon the following Saturday to broadcast the Iowa-Minnesota game at Iowa City.

The Davenport *Democrat and Leader* newspaper reviewed Dutch's account of the game, which was played in a downpour, saying, "His crisp account of the muddy struggle sounded like a carefully written story of the gridiron goings-on, and his quick tongue seemed to be as fast as the plays."

MacArthur liked the broadcast so well that he hired Dutch for three more games, raising his pay to $10 a game. And early the next year, MacArthur took Dutch on as a staff announcer for WOC at a salary of $75 a month.

Although Dutch excelled in describing football games and other sports events, his lack of experience showed whenever he was called upon to read commercials or other material. He didn't sound convincing.

But Dutch found that if he memorized a script and then repeated it aloud before delivering it, the words sounded natural and persuasive. He would later apply the same technique to political speeches.

Dutch moved to Davenport and rented an apartment there. His romance with Mugs Cleaver had ended. During the time he had been pursuing an announcing job, he had neglected her. Mugs, who had become a high-school teacher in a small town in Illinois, sent back the engagement ring that Dutch had given her.

By this time, 1932 was in the history books. Dutch Reagan was on his way.

One day not long after he had joined the staff of WOC in Davenport, Dutch was called into the office of his boss, Peter MacArthur. MacArthur was on the telephone. He was talking with someone at WOC's sister station, WHO in Des Moines.

When Dutch entered the room, MacArthur put his hand over the receiver and said, "Do you know about track?"

Dutch nodded yes.

MacArthur spoke into the phone, "O.K.," he said. "We've got the man."

During the mid-1930s, Reagan's voice was well known through-out the Midwest.

A week later, Dutch was sent to Des Moines, about 150 miles to the west, to broadcast the Drake relays, one of the nation's most noted track events, for WHO. At the time, WHO was building a powerful transmitter that would enable listeners throughout the Midwest to hear its broadcasts. The WHO studios were spacious and modern. Dutch was impressed. This was the big time.

In the months that followed, Dutch was assigned to cover track meets, swimming meets, and football games for WHO. His name and voice became well known to Midwest radio listeners.

Broadcasting in the early 1930s was much more easygoing than it is today. Dutch liked it that way.

One Friday evening, Dutch was on duty at the station. He had thirty minutes of air time to fill with recorded music.

Since the next day was a Saturday and Dutch would be broadcasting a football game, he picked college songs for the records he played. Between records, he made predictions on the games. The executives of the station liked the program so much that they made the show a regular Friday night feature.

During one of the Friday night shows, Dutch's brother, Moon, who happened to be visiting him in Des Moines, was seated in the studio. On one of Dutch's predictions, Moon shook his head in disagreement. The next time he did it, Dutch pushed a microphone in front of him and asked him why he disagreed. Moon explained.

The program continued with the two brothers discussing each prediction. On some they agreed; on others their opinions differed. They promised the audience that they would report which one had the best percentage of correct predictions the following week.

The program opened a door for Moon. It led to his getting a job as a fill-in for Dutch, doing a football scoreboard show on Saturday nights when Dutch was out of town for football broadcasts. And that, in turn, led to Moon's being hired as a staff announcer at WOC after he graduated from Eureka. He later became a program director for WOC, then a producer of network radio shows, and, still later, a highly successful Los Angeles advertising executive.

Dutch was assigned by station WHO to broadcast the home games of the Chicago Cubs and the Chicago White Sox. But the station did not send him to either Wrigley Field or Comiskey Park, the home fields of those teams, to describe the action. Instead, the station relied on a telegraphic re-creation of each game, as did many stations of the day.

It worked like this: In the press box at the ballpark at the stadium in Chicago, a telegraph operator would tap out in Morse code a pitch-by-pitch account of the game. It would be received by another telegraph operator at the WHO studios. The WHO operator, sitting on the opposite side of a glass partition from Dutch, would type out the message and slide it to him through a slot in the window.

Although the message contained only the barest facts,

Dutch would weave the facts into a colorful story. For example, the message handed to Dutch might read: "S2C." From that, Dutch would say, "It's a called strike breaking over the inside corner, making it two strikes on the batter."

He then would rely on his imagination to describe the batter stepping out of the box and tapping dirt from his spikes, and the pitcher dusting his hands on the rosin bag, stepping back onto the mound, looking for the sign, and going into his windup.

Dutch re-created more than 600 games in this fashion during his career. One stands out in his memory.

The Cubs were playing the St. Louis Cardinals. The game was scoreless in the ninth inning. Dizzy Dean was pitching for the Cards. Bill Jurges, the Cubs' shortstop, came to the plate.

Dutch described Dizzy Dean as he went into his windup and sent the ball rocketing toward home plate. Dutch reached for the slip from the engineer, then stared at the message in disbelief. "The wire's gone dead," it read.

Dutch had the ball on the way to the plate. He had no way to call it back. But he reacted quickly. He described Jurges as fouling off a pitch.

Dutch looked at the engineer helplessly. The engineer shrugged.

Dutch didn't want to tell his listeners that there had been an equipment failure. There were several other stations doing broadcasts similar to his. If the audience were to learn that Dutch had lost contact with the ballpark, they would quickly dial another station.

Dutch had Jurges foul a pitch into the box seats. He described in detail two kids scrambling for the ball.

He had Jurges foul another ball behind third and another into the upper deck. Still another was almost a home run. In telling the story in later years, Reagan said he set a world record for successive fouls.

Dutch was beginning to sweat when he looked at the

engineer, saw him suddenly sit up straight and start typing. The ordeal, which had lasted almost seven minutes, was over.

Dutch reached over, grabbed the message, and read it. He could hardly keep from bursting out with a laugh. It said, "Jurges popped out on the first ball pitched."

5

Hollywood

The nation was still in the midst of the Depression, but it hardly seemed to have any effect on Dutch Reagan. He was prospering. By 1936, he was earning $90 a week, a princely sum for the day. He received extra money for speaking at banquets, for writing a sports column for a local newspaper, and for acting as the public-address announcer at games the station did not broadcast.

Dutch had his eye on a Nash convertible he had spotted in the showroom of a Des Moines automobile dealer. When he had saved enough, he paid cash for the car.

Dutch sent money home regularly. His father had suffered a series of heart attacks and was no longer able to work. The money from Dutch enabled his mother to quit her job as a seamstress.

Although he was wonderfully successful, Dutch's dreams for the future went beyond Des Moines. He clung to a vague idea that he might one day become an actor. In 1936, Gene Autry, a cowboy singing star on radio and in the movies, signed a country-and-western group that had appeared on WHO to a motion picture contract. The group was named the Oklahoma Outlaws. The incident started Dutch's mind churning. "If that group can go to Hollywood," he thought, "maybe I can go, too."

One thing that Dutch didn't like about Des Moines was the Iowa winters. They made it difficult for him to enjoy what had become one of his favorite pastimes—horseback riding.

Dutch figured out the way to escape the snow and frigid temperatures. In February each year, the Chicago Cubs journeyed to Catalina Island, just off the southern California coast, to train for the baseball season ahead. Dutch convinced the station management at WHO to send him along to Catalina to cover the Chicago team.

In the winter of 1937 on his trip to Catalina, Dutch took time out to visit the Oklahoma Outlaws. The one-time WHO country-and-western group weren't the only people Dutch knew in Hollywood. He also visited Joy Hodges, a singer from Des Moines who had once worked at WHO. Now she was doing film work and singing with a big band. Dutch told Joy about his ambition to become an actor.

"I know an agent who will be honest with you," Joy said. "If you're wrong [about being an actor], and you should forget the idea, he'll tell you."

Joy arranged the meeting for Dutch with the agent, Bill Meiklejohn. But before she did, she made Dutch get rid of his horn-rimmed glasses. "Don't let him see you with those glasses on," she said.

The next day, Dutch went to see Meiklejohn, who asked him questions about his experience as an actor. Dutch puffed up what he had done. And when Meiklejohn asked him what his salary was, Dutch doubled it.

Stretching the truth didn't do Dutch any harm. Meiklejohn took a liking to the pleasant young man from Des

Moines. He called Warner Brothers, one of the major film studios of the day, and got a casting director there to agree to give Dutch a screen test.

A few days later, Dutch went before the cameras, playing a scene from *Holiday,* a play by Philip Barry. When he had completed the screen test, Dutch was told it would be several days before studio executives would see it. "Stick around," he was told.

"No," said Dutch, explaining that spring training was over for the Cubs and the team was heading back East the next day. Dutch said he intended to be on the train with them. The casting director was impressed by Dutch's coolness.

On the day Dutch arrived in Des Moines, he received a telegram from Bill Meiklejohn that read:

WARNER'S OFFERING CONTRACT FOR SEVEN YEARS, ONE YEAR'S OPTIONS, STARTING AT $200 A WEEK. WHAT SHALL I DO?

Dutch's reply said:

SIGN BEFORE THEY CHANGE THEIR MINDS.

Late in the spring of 1937, twenty-six-year-old Dutch Reagan packed his belongings, said his good-byes, and headed West in his new Nash convertible. He remembers crossing the burning desert and the great stretches of orange groves all the way from San Bernardino to Los Angeles. Today those groves are gone, replaced by housing developments.

Not long after he arrived, Dutch met with executives at Warner Brothers to decide what name he should use in films. Reagan was known as Dutch by everyone, but the studio brass did not think Dutch Reagan was a suitable name for an actor. Reagan himself suggested Ronald Reagan.

Several of the executives seated at the table repeated the name. Finally, the casting director said, "I like it." Everyone else agreed.

Ronald Reagan he was to become once more. As Lou Cannon noted in his book, *Reagan,* many actors and actresses who migrate to Hollywood lose their names, but the young sports announcer from Iowa got his back.

At the time Reagan arrived in Hollywood, the motion picture studios were alive with activity. They had survived the worst days of the Depression, when great portions of their audiences had vanished, and were beginning to turn out films on an assembly line basis—prison pictures, gangster pictures, newspaper pictures, adventure pictures, and backstage musicals.

During the late 1930s, a boy or girl of twelve or younger could go to the movies for a dime. For an adult, admission was a quarter.

The ticket you bought entitled you to sit in the theater for more than three hours and see two feature films, a cartoon, an episode of an adventure serial, a newsreel, and the previews of the six or seven feature films that were to be shown the following week.

The feature films were of two types—A and B. A movies offered the brightest stars and best screenplays. Sometimes A movies were shot in color.

Although the A movie was what brought the audience to the theater, they would stay to watch the B movie as well. The movies churned out Bs quickly and cheaply, sometimes producing them in as few as three or four weeks.

Warner Brothers was fairly typical of most studios of the day. The writers sat in their tiny offices producing scripts, which contained the dialogue and instructions for camera movements. The producers took the scripts and worked out the budgets and cast the leading roles. The directors supervised the filming of the scripts.

During the 1930s, Warner Brothers could boast of a good

number of box office successes. These included musicals such as *Forty-second Street* and *Gold Diggers of 1933*, gangster films like *Little Caesar* and *Public Enemy*, and adventure movies such as *The Charge of the Light Brigade* and *Captain Blood*.

Reagan had been in Hollywood only a few days when he was cast in his first movie, *Love Is on the Air*, a B movie. Before production began, the studio makeup department changed the part in Reagan's hair from the center to the right side of his head.

In the movie, Reagan played the role of a brash young radio announcer who is demoted because of pressure by local businessmen who are in partnership with the racketeers he is trying to expose. The announcer tricks the racketeers into confessing before an open microphone, and wins back his job.

A press book produced by Warner Brothers containing "selling ideas" to advertise and publicize *Love Is on the Air* spoke of Reagan in glowing terms: "We think our new film find will click O.K. because he has an informal, refreshing and engaging manner."

The press book also said, "He knows how to sell himself and his first picture, too!"

Love Is on the Air was the forerunner of many "good guy" roles that Reagan would be handed during the next few years. Often he was cast as a noble-spirited announcer or reporter. He has often described most of his early films as the kind in which he rushed into a room, his hat on the back of his head, grabbed a telephone, and shouted, "Give me the city desk—I've got a story that will crack this town wide open!"

Although he was not one of Hollywood's leading players, Reagan was always very serious-minded about his career. He quickly learned the techniques of acting before a camera: where to stand, what to wear (B performers had to furnish their own wardrobes), and how to kiss ("Your lips should barely touch . . ." he noted in his autobiography. "If you really kiss a girl, it shoves her face out of shape.")

Reagan memorized his scripts quickly, a skill that was well suited to the fast-paced techniques of B-picture-making. He always showed up on time. He made no demands.

He was a "nice guy"—handsome, trustworthy, easygoing.

The producers liked him. As soon as he finished one film, they'd cast him in another.

Following *Love Is on the Air*, Reagan made *Sergeant Murphy*, the story of a calvary horse smuggled into England to become a champion racer. He made *Submarine D-1*, a movie starring Pat O'Brien. Out of this experience, he developed a lifelong friendship with O'Brien, a star of the first rank. Reagan had a role in *Hollywood Hotel*, a major film that featured Dick Powell, another leading star. Reagan became good friends with Powell, too.

Reagan had been in Hollywood only a few months when he decided to send for his mother and father. He put them up in a hotel until he could find an apartment for them. "I need you here," he told them.

He realized that it could be harmful for them to sit around feeling useless, so he put his father in charge of answering his fan mail, which, with the release of his first picture, was beginning to arrive in volume. He saw to it that his father was furnished with a pass to the studio, so that he could work with the mail department in ordering photos and stationery.

Often, on Sunday evenings, Reagan would show up at a Hollywood restaurant named LaRue's for dinner, not with a starlet, but with his mother and father. That was a Hollywood rarity: a good-looking young bachelor who spent so much time with his parents.

In fact, Reagan turned his back on the exotic Hollywood nightlife. His best friends were mostly people he had known in Iowa who, like himself, had come West to pursue their careers.

Reagan's mother and father grew to love California. When

Moon moved to Los Angeles to work in radio, the entire Reagan family was together again.

In 1938, Reagan made eight movies. The last, *Brother Rat*, was an A film in which he had a featured role. It concerned three cadets at the Virginia Military Institute.

In the film, Reagan portrayed a cadet who falls in love with the daughter of the commanding officer of the military academy. The daughter was played by Jane Wyman.

Reagan found the blonde actress very attractive. Like Reagan, she was from a small town in the Midwest—St. Joseph, Missouri. Her family had headed West during the Depression.

In Hollywood, Jane Wyman had first been cast as a dancer in a series of musicals. At the time she met Reagan, she was usually seen portraying a pert, wisecracking comedienne, the leading lady's chum.

Reagan did not date Jane Wyman during the filming of *Brother Rat* because she was going through a divorce. But the following year, 1939, the two began to see each other frequently. They grew closer and closer. They were married on January 26, 1940. Reagan was almost twenty-nine; his bride was twenty-eight. Their wedding reception was a gift from Louella Parsons, a leading gossip columnist of the day.

Warner Brothers tried to capitalize on the Reagan-Wyman marriage by casting them as husband and wife in a comedy, *Angel from Texas*. The movie was not a hit.

By early 1940, Reagan had made twenty movies. He had always done whatever Warner Brothers had told him to do. Now, for the first time, he decided to go after a role that *he* wanted, a role that would provide an escape from B pictures.

He had learned that the studio was soon to begin filming *Knute Rockne—All American*, the life story of the legendary Notre Dame football coach. Pat O'Brien was to portray Rockne.

The role that Reagan wanted was that of George Gipp—the Gipper—an exceptionally talented young football star who had died of pneumonia two weeks after his last game.

Many years after Gipp's death, Rockne, in a dramatic dressing room scene, asks the team to win one for the Gipper, revealing for the first time that this was a request that Gipp had made on his deathbed.

When he became a public figure, and even president, "Win one for the Gipper," always delivered with a grin, became a slogan of Reagan's.

Reagan thought he would be perfect for the role of Gipp, but Warner Brothers, unable to see him as a football player, had no plans to use him in the part. Reagan launched a campaign to get the role. He showed the executive producer photographs of himself in a football uniform that had been taken at Eureka. He got Pat O'Brien to put in a word for him. Reagan eventually got the part.

Reagan had a joyous time making the film. His performance was regarded as one of his best.

When the movie opened, it was a national event. Eighteen states declared the first week in October 1940 Knute Rockne Week. A spectacular opening was held at South Bend, Indiana, home of Notre Dame University.

President Franklin D. Roosevelt, in the midst of his campaign for an unprecedented third term, sent his son and namesake, Franklin D. Roosevelt Jr., to the festivities to represent him. A train with two special cars for the stars carried the Reagans and Pat O'Brien to the premiere. Reagan's father was one of the invited guests. He and Pat O'Brien formed a close friendship which lasted until Mr. Reagan's death a few months after his return to Los Angeles.

Reagan's successful portrayal of George Gipp in the Knute Rockne film marked a turning point in his career, leading to major roles. "Upper-crust picture making" is what Reagan once called it.

Reagan tunes up for his role in Knute Rockne—All American.

He starred with Errol Flynn in *Sante Fe Trail* and with Lionel Barrymore and Wallace Beery in *The Bad Man*. Three other films of Reagan's were released in 1941, all of them earning good reviews. His salary had been boosted to $1000 a week. Real stardom seemed just around the corner.

His popularity with the fans kept escalating. In 1941, Warner's announced that, with the exception of Errol Flynn, Reagan was receiving more fan mail than any other Warner's star. James Cagney was one of those who trailed Reagan.

Speaking of Reagan, the *Los Angeles Times* declared: "His case is very typical of the skyrocketing that happens when a star begins to hit, and it will behoove Warner's to set about getting good roles for Mr. Reagan . . ."

Reagan was rewarded by being cast in what many observers believe to be his best role, that of Drake McHugh in *King's Row*. Ann Sheridan played the female lead.

The McHugh role tested Reagan, for the character was more roguish than any he had portrayed in the past. In the film's climactic scene, McHugh awakens from surgery in which his legs have been amputated by a mad surgeon.

In his hospital bed, when he reaches down and grasps his thighs, and comes to the horror-filled realization of what has happened, McHugh screams, *"Where's the rest of me?"*

Reagan uttered the scream with such conviction that members of the crew filming the scene were brought to tears. (Reagan later used the line as the title for his autobiography.)

Most reviewers praised Reagan for his splendid performance in the film. Reagan himself has called *King's Row* his finest picture.

Before the release of *King's Row*, Warner Brothers rewrote Reagan's contract, increasing his salary from $1000 to $3500 a week.

On January 4, 1941, the Reagans became parents for the first time with the birth of a daughter in Los Angeles.

Promotional movie posters from two of Reagan's films.

Maureen Elizabeth became well known to readers of fan magazines. They wrote about her first spanking, her two pet dogs, and the time she called a kindly woman an old goat.

After *King's Row*, Reagan signed to star with Ann Sheridan in *Juke Girl*, a forgettable film. He followed that with *Desperate Journey*, about a gallant group of airmen flying for Great Britain's Royal Air Force in the early stages of World War II.

On the morning of December 7, 1941, Japanese bombers attacked Pearl Harbor. The next day, the United States declared war on the Axis powers—Japan, Germany, and Italy.

Not long after, while filming *Desperate Journey*, Reagan received a letter from the War Department in Washington that was marked: IMMEDIATE ACTION, ACTIVE DUTY. The letter ordered him to report to Fort Mason in San Francisco. Although he had been placed on limited-service status because of his poor eyesight, Reagan was about to be called into the U.S. Army Air Corps.

6

Lieutenant Reagan

Commissioned as a second lieutenant in the Army Air Corps, Ronald Reagan began his service career at the Fort Mason Port of Embarkation in San Francisco. He was there only a short time before being transferred to the First Motion Picture Unit of the Air Corps, which had taken over the Hal Roach motion picture studios in Burbank.

The 1300 officers and men who made up the unit turned out documentaries and training films, and also conducted a training school for combat cameramen. In the years that followed his Army career, when Reagan would make a personal appearance, TV cameramen or newspaper photographers would often come up to him to tell him they had learned their trade at the Burbank school.

His Army career was no hardship for Reagan. He was able to live at home and drive to work each morning. Although he was used frequently to narrate Army training films, he confessed to getting "more than my share of boredom" during his stay in the Army.

Being in the Army didn't mean that Reagan had to shut

Reagan leaves to report for active duty as lieutenant in the U.S. Army. Actress Jane Wyman (his wife at that time) and their daughter, Maureen Elizabeth, see him off.

down his movie career entirely. He played in a number of short subjects, including *Hollywood in Uniform*, with Clark Gable, Tyrone Power, Alan Ladd, and other stars who were in one branch or another of the armed services.

In 1943, Reagan was detached from the training film unit to play a role in *This Is the Army*, a wartime musical written by Irving Berlin, a well-known songwriter. Since it was a military assignment, he received his first lieutenant's pay of $250 a month. The New York *Times* described the film as "the freshest, the most endearing, the most rousing musical tribute to the American fighting man that has come out of World War II." Warner Brothers turned over all the income it derived from the film to the Army Emergency Relief Fund.

During this time, Reagan was becoming involved with union affairs through his membership in the Screen Actors Guild (SAG). He had joined the union in 1938.

Some actors wanted no part of the union and its politics, believing that it would hurt their careers. But Reagan enjoyed being a member of an organization that was dedicated to helping fellow actors.

He busied himself with union affairs even during the filming of *This Is the Army*. "I never got to know him well," Rosemary DeCamp, who played Reagan's mother in the movie, once recalled. "He was a great negotiator and he was very involved with SAG. He was always rushing onto the set for a few takes, then off somewhere to negotiate something."

When Reagan was discharged from the Army in September 1945 as a captain, he once again earned $3500 a week at Warner Brothers. But aside from *This Is the Army*, his career had been at a virtual standstill for three years. It needed the lift a good role would give it.

While Reagan's career was merely limping along, his wife's was flourishing. In 1945, Jane Wyman earned warm praise for her portrayal of the wife of a writer who was an alcoholic in *The Lost Weekend*. (In March that same year, the Reagans adopted a newborn boy, Michael Edward.) In 1947, Jane Wyman won an Academy Award nomination for her performance in *The Yearling*.

Reagan's first postwar film was *Stallion Road*, in which he played a hero veterinarian. The movie was a financial flop. Reagan followed *Stallion Road* with *That Hagen Girl*, which featured onetime child star Shirley Temple. This too was a box office failure.

Reagan's next film represented a change of pace, a comedy role in the boy-meets-girl tale, *The Voice of the Turtle*. Reagan was amiable and competent, but Eleanor Parker, who played the female lead, walked away with all the best reviews.

During this period, Reagan was becoming more deeply involved with the Screen Actors Guild. The film industry was having serious labor problems. Many studio employees felt they were underpaid. The various craft unions went on strike for more pay and better working conditions.

Things kept getting worse. On October 7, 1945, riots broke out. The strike ended later that month, but flared up again the following year. There were skirmishes between the police and pickets at both Warner Brothers and Metro-Goldwyn-Mayer (MGM).

At about the same time that labor peace returned to Hollywood, the House of Representatives' Un-American Activities Committee announced an investigation into what the committee called "Communist infiltration into the movie industry." The investigation took place during a time of growing hostility between the United States and the Soviet Union.

Robert Taylor, Robert Montgomery, Gary Cooper, and George Murphy were among the Hollywood stars called upon to testify before the committee. Reagan, in his role as an officer of the Screen Actors Guild, was also scheduled to appear as a witness.

On the day the hearings opened, spectators began lining

up at the walnut-paneled doors of the caucus room several hours before the witness was to be called. While Reagan was not a star of the caliber of Robert Taylor or Gary Cooper, he was younger than they were, and his appearance caused a stir. *Newsweek* magazine reported: "Despite his thirty-six years, the pink-cheeked and sandy-haired Ronald Reagan looked so boyish that when he arose to speak, the room was filled with oohs and aahs."

Most of the witnesses agreed that the Communists in Hollywood were very few in number, representing a minority of one percent or less. But it was stressed that they were well organized, extremely active, and very troublesome.

Reagan won praise for his testimony. He agreed that Communists had sought to control the film industry. But he argued that no measures or methods beyond those of vigorous and democratic union activity were needed to turn aside the Communist threat.

"In the Screen Actors Guild," said Reagan, "we make it work by insuring everyone a vote and by keeping everyone informed. I believe that, as Thomas Jefferson put it, if all the American people know all of the facts they will never make a mistake."

Reagan's testimony impressed many people. He was hailed because of his fairness and because he had not resorted to name calling.

Later that year, Reagan was elected president of the Screen Actors Guild. He was to be elected to five consecutive one-year terms as its president. In 1949 and 1950, Reagan also served as chairman of the Motion Picture Industry Council, an organization dedicated to improving the public image of the film business.

Jane Wyman was just as busy as her husband. Following her successes in *The Lost Weekend* and *The Yearling*, she was cast as a deaf-mute in *Johnny Belinda*, a role for which she won an Oscar as best actress. There was no question about it now—Reagan's wife was the star of the family.

A 1947 photo of the president, listening to testimony at the October 22 session of the House Un-American Activities Committee investigation in Washington, D.C.

When the filming of *Johnny Belinda* was completed, she announced she wanted to go to New York City to visit friends, and that she wanted to go alone. "There's no use lying," she told a reporter. "I'm not the happiest girl in the world."

Reagan admitted to columnist Hedda Hopper that there were problems in their marriage. "We had a tiff," he told her. "But we've had tiffs before, as what couple married eight years hasn't. But I expect that when Janie gets back we'll get back together all right."

The Reagans were a couple with few similarities. He was open and optimistic; she was intense and restless. He was deeply interested in the Screen Actors Guild and union politics; she wasn't. He liked sports; she liked night-clubbing.

In February 1948, Jane Wyman announced that she was filing for a divorce. At the court hearing, she testified that Reagan's position as president of the Screen Actors Guild had led to his having such an absorbing interest in politics that there finally was "nothing to sustain our marriage."

The divorce decree became final in July 1949. Reagan's wife was granted custody of the two children, Maureen, then eight, and Michael, four.

"The problem hurt our children most," Reagan wrote in his autobiography. "There is no easy way to break up a home, and I don't think there is any way to ease the bewildered pain of children at such times."

7

Nancy

Reagan's divorce was not the only thing to bring him distress. His film career was also beginning to cause him pain.

Late in 1948, Warner Brothers sent Reagan to England to film *The Hasty Heart*. Except for a few scenes, the entire motion picture took place in a hospital ward. Reagan played Yank, a wounded but jovial American who tries to befriend a hostile Scotsman. Patricia Neal was a sympathetic nurse.

The Hasty Heart took almost four months to make. Reagan disliked English food and hated English weather. "Our wardrobe for the entire picture was either pajamas or shorts," he said, "and we froze most of the time."

He missed his children. It was a gloomy winter for him.

One thing buoyed his spirits. One of his ambitions was to star in a major Western film, and he had been successful in getting Warner Brothers to purchase a Western story for him. It was titled *Ghost Mountain*. Reagan looked forward to returning to Hollywood and starting work on the film.

In the spring of 1949 when the production work on *The Hasty Heart* was completed, Reagan boarded the passenger liner *Queen Mary* for his return trip to the United States. On the day the ship landed in New York, Reagan read an article in *Variety*, the show business newspaper, saying that *Ghost Mountain* was going into production, but that the film was to star not himself, but Errol Flynn.

Reagan was livid. He felt he had been betrayed. He began a heated feud with the studio bosses at Warner's. As a result of the battle, his agent negotiated a new contract for him. It cut the number of films he would make for Warner Brothers but enabled him to work for other companies. Previously he had been under exclusive contract to Warner's.

Shortly after, Reagan signed to do a series of films for Universal Pictures. The first was a thriller, *Fugitive from Terror*.

But before Reagan could begin work on the film, misfortune struck. He was taking part in a charity baseball game between leading men and comedians at the old Wrigley Field in Los Angeles. In the first inning, while streaking down the line toward first base, he collided with another player. Reagan went down in a thick cloud of dust and didn't get up. He was carried from the field on a stretcher. X rays later revealed he had broken his right thigh in six places.

Reagan spent the next eight weeks in the hospital and he hobbled around on crutches for months. His part in *Fugitive from Terror* went to another actor. Reagan prayed that one day he would regain full use of his leg.

Reagan had always thought of himself as an actor, but now his acting career seemed to be slipping away. He had thought of himself as a husband and father, but now he had no wife or family. These were bleak days for Reagan.

One day in the fall of 1949, Reagan received a telephone call from producer-director Mervyn LeRoy. LeRoy had been responsible for more than a score of successful films, including *The Wizard of Oz*, which he had produced.

LeRoy wanted a favor. In a picture he was then working on, *East Side, West Side*, there was an actress named Nancy Davis. She was very much distressed because the name Nancy Davis kept showing up on a Communist mailing list. To be identified as a Communist in those days could ruin one's career. Since Reagan was president of the Screen Actors Guild, LeRoy wanted him to call Nancy Davis and discuss the problem with her.

Reagan checked into the matter. He discovered that she had been confused with another actress who had the same name. LeRoy arranged a dinner meeting so that Reagan could explain the mix-up to Nancy.

Nancy Davis was already twenty-eight years old when she met Ronald Reagan. She had been born in 1921 in New York City. Her parents, a car salesman named Kenneth Robbins and an actress named Edith Luckett, split up the same year.

Edith toured in plays to support herself and her daughter. The toddler was entrusted to the care of Edith's sister, Virginia Galbraith, who lived in Bethesda, Maryland.

In 1929, Edith was married a second time, to Loyal Davis, a successful Chicago surgeon. Nancy was reclaimed from Aunt Virginia. It was the start of a new life for her. Growing up was a happy time of parties and nice clothes. During the summers, she went to camp and on vacation trips with relatives and friends. At age fourteen Dr. Davis legally adopted her, and she became Nancy Davis.

In school, she played field hockey and was a leader in student government. She took part in school dramatics and had the lead in the senior play, *First Lady*.

At Smith College in Northampton, Massachusetts, she majored in drama and dated a lot. She also gained more acting experience as a member of a summer stock company.

Most members of the class of 1943 went from graduation to marriage. Not Nancy. She returned to Chicago to stay with her mother (her adoptive father was serving with the

U.S. Army in Europe), and worked as a clerk in a department store and as a nurse's aide in a hospital.

With the encouragement of her mother, she landed a role with a touring company in the play *Ramshackle Inn.* That led to a part on Broadway, some television work, and eventually a contract with MGM.

Moviegoers first saw Nancy Davis in 1949 as the gentle daughter in *The Doctor and the Girl,* with Glenn Ford and Janet Leigh. But becoming a successful Hollywood actress was not Nancy's ultimate goal. Her "greatest ambition," she wrote in an MGM biographical questionnaire, was "to have a successful, happy marriage."

Ronald Reagan was probably not the kind of man she had dreamed of marrying. Although he looked younger, he was thirty-nine when they first met (and was still getting around on crutches as the result of his broken leg). His last important picture, *King's Row,* had been filmed several years before. He was a divorced man with two children whose former wife was probably better known than he was. Indeed, Jane Wyman's photograph always seemed to be staring up at Nancy from the covers of fan magazines.

Nancy continued to see other men after her first date with Reagan, and he continued to date other women. On weekends, he would often take his children Maureen and Michael to a small ranch he had purchased in Northridge, California, not far from Los Angeles. There he let them ride two gentle horses he had bought for them. Reagan later purchased a 290-acre ranch in the Santa Monica Mountains north of Los Angeles.

Once Reagan's broken leg had healed (the leg never totally regained its flexibility), he began working in motion pictures again. He filmed *Louisa,* a comedy for Universal Pictures, and *Storm Warning,* a crusading movie about the Ku Klux Klan.

His most noted film of this period was *Bedtime for Bonzo,*

in which he shared the screen with a mischief-making chimpanzee. Reagan portrayed a psychology professor whose father had a criminal record. The professor sets out to prove that environment, not heredity, is the most decisive factor in molding a person's character. He borrows the chimp, Bonzo, for the experiment. *Motion Picture* magazine said of the film: "The movie is merry, the acting energetic. Nobody proves anything and Bonzo earns all the laughs."

Bedtime for Bonzo is often revived by local television stations. Political opponents of Reagan's have used the film to poke fun at him.

The same year—1951—Reagan fulfilled one of his long-time ambitions when he finally got to work in a Western, *The Last Outpost*. It told the story of Confederate soldiers trying to capture gold being shipped West.

Nancy Davis was busy in films, too. Before she married, she had made eight movies and was praised by the New York *Herald-Tribune* for her "good, solid acting."

Nancy Davis and Ronald Reagan were often an "item" in Hollywood gossip columns. They dined at Chasen's, a well-known Hollywood restaurant frequented by the stars, and they often spent quiet evenings with their friends, William and Ardis Holden, at their Toluca Lake home. William Holden was a leading actor of the day.

On March 4, 1952, when Nancy Davis and Ronald Reagan were married at the Little Brown Church in the Valley, Bill Holden was the best man and his wife the matron of honor. After their marriage, the Reagans lived in Nancy's apartment and later bought a small house in Pacific Palisades.

A daughter, Patricia Ann, was born to the Reagans on October 22, 1952, and a son, Ronald Prescott, was born on May 28, 1958.

Nancy Reagan, according to Lou Cannon in *Reagan*, became the "spark and drive" in her husband's life. At the same time, she was "his comforter," providing a secure retreat from which he could go forth each day to do battle with Hollywood producers, directors, and studio heads; and later, campus protestors, liberals, Democrats—anyone.

She was always there to support him, to guide him. According to most observers, Nancy Reagan played a critical role in the success he was later to achieve.

Ronald Reagan weds Nancy Davis.

8

Transition

For Hollywood, the 1950s was a decade of change. Television had become an important force, causing audiences and box office receipts to shrink. The movie industry tried to think up ways to compete against the monster box in everyone's living room.

The 1950s was a decade of change for Ronald Reagan, too. The number of his movie appearances decreased. He made his last Warner Brothers film in 1952 *(She's Working Her Way Through College)*. He was cast in two films in 1953, one at Paramount Pictures *(Tropic Zone)* and another at Universal Studios *(Law and Order)*. In 1954, he had the lead in a low-budget film at MGM *(Prisoner of War)*.

Reagan fully realized he had no future in motion pictures. Although he had often spoken out against television, which he thought was ruining the motion picture business, when an opportunity in TV presented itself, Reagan grabbed it.

Late in 1954, Reagan was approached by Taft Schreiber, head of MCA, the giant entertainment complex, and asked whether he might be interested in becoming the host of a new television series that was to be sponsored by General

Electric, a leading manufacturer of electrical products. Reagan said yes. The job was to pay him a yearly salary of $125,000, later to be increased to $150,000.

"The GE Theater," as the series was titled, was one of the best weekly drama series in the history of television. It was also one of the most popular, ranking among television's top twenty programs week after week from 1954 to 1962.

In his role as host of "The GE Theater," Reagan introduced such stars as Joan Crawford, Alan Ladd, and Fred Astaire. He also starred in some of the dramas. In one, "A Turkey for the President," telecast on Thanksgiving Day, 1960, he played opposite Nancy.

At the same time he was working on "The GE Theater," Reagan appeared in more feature films. In 1957, he made *Hellcats of the Navy*. He starred as the commanding officer of a World War II submarine who was engaged to a Navy nurse played by Nancy.

Hellcats of the Navy was Reagan's fifty-second feature film. Most observers credit Reagan with a fifty-third feature, *The Killers*, produced in 1964. This, however, was a made-for-television movie that was released to motion picture theaters because it was considered too violent for the home screen. In *The Killers*, Reagan played a bad guy, the only time in his long career that he did so. *The Killers* was the last feature film in which Reagan appeared.

As part of his agreement with General Electric, Reagan toured the country three months a year, meeting company executives and employees, and plugging GE toasters, TV sets, and other products.

He met office workers; he toured labs and assembly lines. He shook hands with members of the night shift.

One plant distributed more than 10,000 photographs of Reagan to its employees, and in two days he signed every one of them. Another time, at a dinner in his honor, he stood in a reception line and shook two thousand hands.

In two of the eight years he was under contract to GE,

Reagan visited every one of the company's 135 plants and met most of its 250,000 employees. Although it was not easy work, Reagan liked it, calling it one of the most enjoyable experiences of his life.

Reagan had long served as a spokesman for the motion picture industry, and when GE found out how skilled he was as a speaker, the company began booking speeches for him. He sometimes delivered as many as fourteen speeches in a day.

Reagan was afraid to fly at that time, so, accompanied by a public-relations representative, he would ride trains from one stop to the next. He used the travel time to work on his speeches, drawing material from his experiences in Hollywood and from what he read in the daily newspaper, the *Saturday Evening Post,* and the *Reader's Digest.*

The content of his speeches went through a period of change. At first, his remarks were usually simply patriotic in nature, and frequently included a defense of Hollywood's manners and morals.

But gradually the content of his speeches began to change, for Reagan himself was changing. He had always been a liberal and a Democrat. He had always favored having government play an active role in the regulation of the economy in the public interest. He had campaigned and voted for candidates who had endorsed government programs meant to provide economic security and ease human suffering. These included such programs as unemployment insurance, health insurance, old-age pensions, and civil-rights legislation.

Reagan's political hero had always been Franklin D. Roosevelt, a Democrat, who was first elected president in 1932 and then reelected three more times. He was the only president elected four times. Roosevelt led the United States through its worst depression and through a World War. Reagan voted for Roosevelt all four times.

Reagan was attracted to Roosevelt's liberal leadership in

the 1930s and 1940s because he believed that Roosevelt was fighting for each person's freedom from want and dependence. He believed that Roosevelt was battling to restore the dignity of the individual.

After Roosevelt, Reagan continued to support Democratic candidates. He had campaigned on radio for President Harry S. Truman and for Senator Hubert H. Humphrey of Minnesota in 1948. He supported Democrat Helen Gahagan Douglas for the U.S. Senate in California against Republican Richard M. Nixon in 1950. Nixon won.

But by the early 1960s, Reagan was more conservative than liberal, more Republican than Democrat. In the 1940s, Reagan had attacked the wealth and power of greedy corporations that undermined the independence of the worker. By the 1960s, Reagan believed the culprit was no longer big business, but government. But the problem was the same—the loss of individual freedom.

Reagan's audiences had helped to change him. He came to realize that he was speaking to people who "were very different than the people Hollywood was talking about," and that he was seeing "the same people he grew up with in Dixon, Illinois." He realized that he "was living in a tinsel factory," and "the exposure brought him back."

Whereas Reagan had seen Franklin D. Roosevelt as the champion of "the forgotten man at the bottom of the economic pyramid in the 1930s," Reagan began to look upon himself as the defender of "the forgotten American, the man out in the suburbs working sixty hours a week to support his family and being taxed heavily for the benefit of someone else."

Newspapers were beginning to refer to Reagan as "a prominent conservative spokesman." He did not disagree. He thought of himself as a patriotic American who was calling attention to the government, a problem so critical that it would destroy the country if it were not corrected.

Early one winter morning in 1962, Reagan arrived in St.

Paul, Minnesota, to ride in the city's annual Winter Carnival Parade and speak at an assembly at Central High School. As he stepped down from the train, someone handed him a local newspaper. Reagan was shocked to read that the Teachers Federation had passed a resolution the night before that demanded he not be permitted to speak to the students because he was a "controversial personality."

Reagan went ahead with the speech anyway. When he was introduced, the students stood and cheered for five minutes.

On another occasion that same year, 1962, Reagan had given his usual speech for General Electric in Bloomington, Illinois, and afterward was branded as "a right-wing extremist" by a labor newspaper. Reagan found it difficult to understand what the newspaper was so upset about.

Some executives at General Electric were beginning to be embarrassed by the conservative nature of Reagan's speeches. One executive called Reagan and asked him to make his speeches less political. He wanted Reagan to speak only on behalf of the company's products. Reagan said he could not do that. Within two days, General Electric canceled "The GE Theater" and Reagan's association with the company.

Reagan was not absent from the TV screen for very long. Soon after the cancellation of "The GE Theater," his brother Neil, who had become a Los Angeles advertising executive, came to him with an offer. One of the advertising accounts at Neil's agency, U.S. Borax, a manufacturer of cleaning products, was seeking a host to introduce their TV program, "Death Valley Days," and serve as a company spokesman. Would Reagan want the job? At first Reagan turned down the offer. Later, however, he changed his mind and accepted it.

In 1962, at the age of fifty-one, Reagan, the onetime liberal Democrat, began crusading for conservative causes.

He spoke out against Communism by playing an active role in Dr. Fred Schwarz's Christian anti-Communist campaign. He became a member of Project Prayer, a Hollywood movement that rallied against the Supreme Court's decision ending prayer in public schools.

In 1964, Reagan campaigned for the Republican candidate for president, Barry Goldwater. Reagan had met Goldwater, a U.S. senator from Arizona, while visiting Nancy's parents at their home in Phoenix. Reagan admired Goldwater for his straightforward brand of conservatism.

For six weeks, as cochairman of the California Republicans for Goldwater, Reagan traveled the state for the candidate, delivering several speeches a day. Reagan himself was a big hit—but his candidate wasn't. President Lyndon B. Johnson, the Democratic candidate, had no trouble portraying Goldwater as a right-wing extremist, a war hawk. Johnson got across the idea that if Goldwater became president, the nation would be imperiled.

On October 27, 1964, a speech that Reagan had pretaped on behalf of Goldwater played on national television. "A Time for Choosing" was its title.

Reagan was in top form as he delivered the speech, the words coming easily and naturally, the tone serious, even intense. He attacked high taxes, wasteful government spending, and growing welfare costs.

He spoke of the threat of Communism, saying, "We cannot buy our security, our freedom from the threat of the bomb, by committing an immorality so great as saying to a billion human beings now in slavery behind the Iron Curtain, 'Give up your dreams of freedom, because to save our own skin, we are willing to make a deal with your slavemasters.'"

In his conclusion, Reagan looked directly into the camera and said: "You and I have a rendezvous with destiny [a phrase he borrowed from Franklin D. Roosevelt]. We can preserve for our children this last best hope of man on

Earth, or we can sentence them to take the first step into a thousand years of darkness. If we fail, at least let our children and our children's children say of us we justified our brief moment here. We did all that can be done."

Goldwater had frightened the voters with his bluntness, his uncompromising attitude. Reagan's ideas were hardly any different than Goldwater's. But Reagan wrapped his ideas in a pretty package. He reassured people; he charmed them. He appealed to their sense of patriotism. Said one of his opponents: "Reagan manages to get away with being a thundering conservative by not thundering."

His speech on behalf of Barry Goldwater worked to transform Ronald Reagan. No longer was he looked upon as a Hollywood actor whose career was fast fading. Now he was considered by many to be the most important conservative politician in America.

9

Governor

Through the years, people had been asking Reagan to run for political office, first for the U.S. House of Representatives as a Democrat and, much later, for the U.S. Senate as a Republican. Now the requests were becoming more frequent and more serious.

Several weeks after the telecast of "A Time for Choosing," a group called the Friends of Ronald Reagan met in California. Their goal: to launch Reagan's candidacy for the office of governor of California.

At one time, it might have seemed odd for a Hollywood actor to run for governor. But not in 1965—not after what had happened to George Murphy. A good friend of Reagan's, Murphy was a song-and-dance man who had been featured in Hollywood musical comedies. He had costarred with Nancy Reagan in *Talk About a Stranger* and played Reagan's father in *This Is the Army*. In 1964, running as a Republican, Murphy won election to the U.S. Senate from California. He was the first professional actor in modern history to be elected to a major political office. If Murphy could do it, Reagan thought, why couldn't he?

Reagan announced he was a candidate for governor in January 1966. But before he could enter the contest against Governor Pat Brown, a Democrat, Reagan had to enter the Republican primary. (In a primary, a party conducts an election among its members. The winner of the primary then faces the candidate representing the opposition party in the general election.)

Reagan's opponent in the Republican primary was Mayor George Christopher of San Francisco. During the campaign, Reagan described himself as a citizen-politician who was eager to clean up the mess in Sacramento, the state capital, and around the state. Christopher failed to get much support. In the election, with over 1.4 million Republicans casting ballots, Reagan received 65 percent of the vote. Reagan's ability as a vote getter had been established.

In the campaign against Governor Pat Brown that followed, Reagan made pleas for freedom and traditional values. He said that big government had become the master instead of the servant. It devoured the hard-earned wages of working men and women. At the same time, it made life easy for welfare cheats—lazy people who freeloaded. It choked free enterprise with regulations and red tape.

The state's problems, Reagan said, grew out of a lack of will; they stemmed from morally lax leaders who allowed convicts to go free. He condemned students at the University of California at Berkeley and other universities who were demonstrating against the Vietnam War.

What Reagan was saying appealed to Californians up and down the state, but particularly to the middle-class suburbanites of the southern regions of the state. Many of them shared Reagan's concerns about high taxes, excessive government, and state aid to minorities.

Reagan's ideas were no more than an echo of what other conservatives had long been saying. But when Brown and his supporters sought to brand Reagan as a right-winger, an extremist, Reagan neatly sidestepped the charge. He came across as sincere and realistic, a man with a friendly interest for the concerns of the voters. He was the "good guy from the old West," said one observer.

Nancy Reagan, who had edged away from show business after her marriage to concentrate on being a wife and mother, took on a new role as a campaigner, appearing mostly before women's groups. She disliked speech making and so relied on a question-and-answer format for most of her appearances.

No one ever doubted that Nancy loved her husband very much. One piece of evidence was "the Gaze"—she would stare up at him in a worshipful manner, usually as he delivered a speech.

Some people said that it was phony, that she was acting. Nancy protested that it was a natural way of watching anyone speak. At any rate, the attention she attracted caused her to tone down the Gaze.

During the final stages of the campaign, the Brown forces produced a television commercial that showed the governor

The president and his first lady.

telling a class of young schoolchildren, "I'm running against an actor, and you know who shot Lincoln, don'tcha?" (This was a reference to John Wilkes Booth, the actor who assassinated President Abraham Lincoln.) The remark backfired and won Reagan countless sympathy votes.

Reagan managed to portray Brown as part of the problem. The high taxes, the big state budgets, the black riots that had taken place in the Watts section of Los Angeles, and the student disorders at Berkeley—Brown was made to shoulder the responsibility for all of these.

Regarding the state budget, Reagan said, "Governor Brown calls it lean and hard, and believe me, that's what he's doing—leanin' hard."

Regarding Democratic president Lyndon B. Johnson's Great Society, a package of social-welfare legislation, Reagan said, "It grows greater every day—greater in cost, greater in inefficiency, and greater in waste."

On election day, Reagan won a smashing victory, polling 3.7 million votes to 2.7 million for Brown. Ronald Reagan's political career was under way.

As governor, Reagan had no problem compromising with legislators when he thought it necessary to compromise. He showed himself to be more practical and restrained than anyone would have judged from his campaign speeches.

Fulfilling his promise "to clean up the mess" at the Berkeley campus of the University of California, Reagan fired the university president and called in the National Guard and Highway Patrol to ensure order on the campus. But later he approved generous increases in the budgets for higher education.

When he learned that he had taken over a state that was in the midst of a financial crisis, he supported multibillion-dollar tax increases. At the same time, he put a freeze on hiring and instituted other economy measures.

Later, when these efforts, plus an improvement in the

state's economy, led to big budget surpluses, he paid out tax rebates and reduced property taxes.

The governor's residence in Sacramento was a gloomy old firetrap on a busy street. The Reagans rented a twelve-room house in a residential neighborhood, and paid the rent— $2500 a month—from their own funds. There Reagan liked to spend quiet evenings with Nancy and their nine-year-old son Ronnie, who was nicknamed Skipper. Thirteen-year-old Patti was away at Orme School in Arizona.

Nancy's interest in clothes and fashion came to the attention of the press. An article in *Life* magazine called her "a walking showcase for California fashion designers." She also spent a good amount of her time visiting wounded veterans of the Vietnam War.

By the end of his first term as governor, Reagan still looked upon himself as a "citizen-politician," battling the social evils of the day. He had little trouble winning reelection.

In his second term, he was more the skilled professional, and he enjoyed being governor more. His major achievement was the California Welfare Reform Act of 1971. This reduced the number of people receiving welfare while boosting payments to what Reagan's administration called the "truly needy."

Reagan also signed into law some measures that were quite liberal. Some people said that Reagan's overall record as governor was noteworthy not so much because it was different from the record of Governor Pat Brown and other Democrats, but because it was similar.

By the middle of 1974, the sixty-three-year-old governor, who had become known for always keeping a jar of jelly beans on his desk for young visitors, made it clear that he did not intend to run a third time. In January 1975, he left office and was succeeded by Edmund "Jerry" Brown, the son of the man he had defeated in 1966.

Presidential Candidate

After Reagan had been governor for about a year, his supporters had convinced him to seek the Republican presidential nomination in 1968. Reagan waited, however, until the opening of the national convention to announce his candidacy, which was a tactical error. By that time, it was too late to stop the nomination of Richard M. Nixon.

In the 1968 presidential election campaign, Nixon narrowly defeated Hubert H. Humphrey, the Democratic nominee, and George Wallace, a third-party candidate. Four years later, in 1972, Nixon, as expected, sought and won the Republican nomination again. He trounced George McGovern in the election campaign that followed.

Traditionally, a presidential incumbent—the person already holding the office—is not opposed for the party's nomination. Reagan saw no reason to buck this tradition in Nixon's case. Reagan was in his second term as governor at the time. He decided he would simply wait until 1976 when, because of the Twenty-second Amendment to the Constitution, Nixon would be unable to seek a third term. Then Reagan would make a serious try for the nomination.

But Reagan's plans went haywire. Nixon never reached the end of his presidential term. Five men were arrested for breaking into the offices of the Democratic National Committee in the Watergate hotel and apartment complex in Washington, D.C., in June 1972. The investigations that followed uncovered the Watergate scandal, leading to Nixon's resignation on August 9, 1974, and to the swearing in of Nixon's vice-president, Gerald Ford, as the thirty-eighth president.

Therefore, when the Republican nominating convention took place in 1976, Gerald Ford would be the incumbent. Ford, by tradition, would be able to seek the nomination without opposition.

After Reagan left office as governor in 1975, he and Nancy moved back to their home in Pacific Palisades, California. They had a new interest now. Only weeks before, they had purchased a 688-acre ranch south of Los Angeles in Riverside County. Located high on a plateau in the Santa Ynez Mountains, looking out toward the Pacific Ocean only thirty-five miles away, it was called Rancho del Cielo (Ranch in the Sky).

Reagan worked hard at renovating the ranch's eighty-seven-year-old two-bedroom house. He was helped by William "Barney" Barnett, who had been his driver and bodyguard during his years as governor. Working on weekends, the two men took down some of the walls, put in a new kitchen and family room, and installed a glass tile roof.

There was much else to keep the Reagans busy. The former governor had left office as a very popular figure and was in hot demand as a speaker, making eight to ten speeches a month (at an average fee of $5000 a speech). He began a weekday radio commentary program and started writing a weekly column that appeared in 174 newspapers.

Newspaper reporters kept asking Reagan whether he was

planning to run against Gerald Ford for the Republican nomination. Reagan insisted he wasn't. He had no wish to divide the Republican party and in so doing perhaps make it easy for a Democrat to win the presidential election of 1976.

But little by little, Reagan began to change his mind. Eventually he decided to challenge the president for the nomination.

The Reagan people did not look at Ford as being a "real" incumbent. He had been appointed by Nixon; he had not been elected as vice-president. (Nixon chose Ford as a replacement for Spiro Agnew, who had resigned after being charged with tax evasion on payments made to him by a Maryland contractor when he was governor of that state.)

But more than that, Reagan and his supporters were upset with Ford because he had made New York governor Nelson Rockefeller his vice-president. Reagan had hoped to be chosen himself. In his eyes, not getting the bid was bad enough. But having the bid go to Rockefeller, who represented the liberal wing of the Republican party, was even worse. The selection angered Republican conservatives.

"Jerry Ford can't cut the mustard," one of Reagan's advisers told him. "He's not perceived as a leader; he can't lead Congress or the country."

Reagan's age was also a factor in his decision to seek the nomination. He celebrated his sixty-fifth birthday in 1976. Many people believed that if he waited until 1980 to seek the nomination, his age would weigh too heavily against him.

By the fall of 1975, it was clear that Reagan was going to run against Ford for the Republican presidential nomination the next summer. By November, he had declared himself a candidate.

For a time, it seemed quite likely that Reagan would emerge as his party's candidate. Looking back, it is difficult to pinpoint exactly what went awry during the campaign and cost him the nomination.

Some observers say that he made a serious mistake during the New Hampshire primary, where he predicted victory and even allowed himself to be photographed smiling and holding a newspaper with a headline reporting that he had won. But Ford beat Reagan in New Hampshire. Reagan lost the primary in his native state of Illinois, too.

Others say Reagan hurt his chances when he selected Pennsylvania Senator Richard Schweicker as his vice-presidential running mate. A liberal on labor issues, Schweicker cost Reagan the support of some conservative-minded delegates.

Whatever the reason, when the Republican delegates gathered at their Kansas City, Kansas, convention early in August 1976, it was Gerald Ford they selected as their candidate. Ford's victory was a narrow one, 1187 delegates to 1070 for Reagan.

When it was over, the Reagans returned to Rancho del Cielo. Reagan resumed his radio broadcasts, his newspaper column, and his speech making. He had lost in Kansas City. But losing there would help to pave the way for the victories that lay ahead.

During Reagan's try for the presidential nomination in 1976, the Reagan children were caught in the spotlight. Maureen, then thirty-five, had attended boarding schools and dropped out of college. She had married twice while in her twenties and had struggled as an actress and singer.

An excellent public speaker, Maureen had become the most politically active of the Reagan children. As a Republican conservative, she had condemned those who demonstrated against the Vietnam War as being Communist-inspired.

Still later, Maureen became a staunch advocate of the Equal Rights Amendment, which stated simply, "Equality of rights under the law shall not be denied or abridged by the United States or any state on account of sex." Although her father opposed passage of the amendment, Maureen pledged to support it "until the day I die."

Michael, then thirty-one, had turned to speedboating as a career. A preschooler when Reagan and Jane Wyman were divorced, he had attended several different high schools and played quarterback well enough to be offered a scholarship to Arizona State University. He turned it down after deciding that college players took the game too seriously. He became a salesman of yachts and pleasure boats in 1971.

Patricia, twenty-four in 1976, used the professional name Patti Davis and was the most defiant of the Reagan children. A former theater arts major at the University of Southern California, she was attempting to launch a career as a singer-actress. During the early 1970s, she lived with rock musician Bernie Leadon of the Eagles, opposed the Vietnam War, and, for a time, had no contact with her mother and father. "I was very rebellious and very feisty," she once recalled.

Ron, then eighteen, was closest to his father and the best

The Reagan clan. From left: Neil Reagan, the president's brother; Dennis Revell, Maureen Reagan's husband; Bess Reagan, Neil's wife; Maureen Reagan; Nancy and Ronald Reagan; Patti Davis; Paul Grilley, Patti's husband; Doria Reagan, Ron Jr.'s wife; and Ron Reagan, Jr.

student of the Reagan children. It upset him that his father was "the guy they loved to hate" at California colleges during the 1970s. "He was portrayed as some kind of an ogre for a long time," Ron said, "and he's such a gentle guy and such a real person, I always wanted to take those people and shake them." A senior at a private school in southern California, where he had become interested in ballet, Ron took a year off to campaign with his father.

Even before the election of 1976, in which Ford was eventually defeated by former Georgia governor Jimmy Carter, Reagan began to plan for 1980. Reagan did campaign for Ford that fall, making appearances in twenty states. Each time he made sure to stress the conservative aspects of the Republican program.

Reagan had $1 million in campaign funds left over from 1976, and he and his advisers used the money to help keep his name before the public. During the period between the 1976 elections and the official opening of his campaign for the nomination in November 1979, Reagan spent about half of his time at Rancho del Cielo and the other half speech making and working on his newspaper column and radio show.

By this time, Reagan had been active on the American political scene for a decade and a half, and he had become a political superstar. Or, as one observer noted, he was "in the major leagues of presidential candidates." The public had such a high awareness of him that they readily accepted him as being presidential in character. Senator Edward "Ted" Kennedy was such a figure among the Democrats. And Gerald Ford had also achieved this lofty ranking among Republicans. But Ford was not expected to try for the nomination in 1980.

Reagan's superstar status gave him a big advantage over the other Republican candidates. These included Representatives John B. Anderson and Philip Crane; Senators Howard H. Baker, Jr., and Robert Dole; former Texas governor John Connally; and former director of the Central Intelligence Agency George Bush.

Bush loomed as the most formidable of Reagan's rivals. He had served in several branches of the government. Besides his experience with the CIA, he had been a Texas congressman, the nation's chief diplomatic representative to China, and U.S. ambassador to the United Nations. Bush, tall and good-looking, was fifty-six, thirteen years younger than Reagan.

Bush became a serious problem for the Reagan forces in the Iowa precinct caucuses of January 21, 1980. He campaigned hard in Iowa, while Reagan darted in and out of the state. Bush was able to say he spent more days in Iowa than Reagan spent hours.

The hard work paid off. Bush won 33 percent of the vote; Reagan got 30 percent. Now Bush was hailed as the campaign's front-runner.

What happened in Iowa was a rude awakening for Reagan. It made him realize that no one was going to hand him the nomination. He was going to have to work for it.

The next important event was the New Hampshire primary. Reagan campaigned as if everything depended on it. During one stretch, he rode on campaign buses for twenty-one consecutive days, stopping for speeches and press conferences, often standing in the freezing cold. He responded warmly to the crowds, answering questions easily and openly. Some reporters half his age became worn out by the grind.

The campaign in New Hampshire reached a dramatic high point with a debate at a Nashua high school one evening a few days before the voting. At first, it was arranged as a two-man debate, Reagan versus Bush. The debate was to be sponsored by the Nashua *Telegraph,* with the costs to be paid by the Reagan campaign committee.

But Reagan's campaign manager decided to invite the

other four candidates to participate in the debate. He did not tell Bush of his decision. On the night of the debate, Reagan welcomed the other candidates. Bush, however, refused to allow the others to participate, saying he had agreed to certain rules in advance and saw no reason to change them. The crowd booed and hissed when Bush announced his stand.

As Bush sat stiffly on the stage, Reagan led the other candidates to the podium. He took the microphone and began explaining why the other candidates should be permitted to speak.

Suddenly the voice of Jon Breen, editor of the *Telegraph*, rang out. "Turn off Mr. Reagan's microphone," he yelled, trying to get control of the proceedings.

Reagan was equal to the moment. "I paid for this microphone," he declared, his voice a mixture of anger and righteousness.

Some reporters said that moment was a turning point in the campaign. Reagan captured the support of the crowd, went on to win the debate that followed, and later walloped Bush and all the other candidates in the balloting.

Reagan's popularity continued to grow by leaps and bounds. In March, he won important primary victories over John Connally in South Carolina and over John B. Anderson and George Bush in Illinois. By the end of May, twenty-four primaries had been held, and Reagan had won twenty of them.

The other Republicans, realizing that they had no chance to win, withdrew from the race. Anderson, however, announced he would run as an independent.

Reagan easily won the nomination on the first ballot at the convention in Detroit, Michigan. At Reagan's request, Bush was nominated as vice-president.

Meanwhile, the Democrats nominated the incumbents, President Jimmy Carter and Vice-President Walter F. Mondale. Now the *real* race would begin.

George Bush had "loomed as the most formidable of Reagan's rivals" in seeking the Republican nomination for president in 1980. The two later became a winning team.

II

Victory

As the election campaign of 1980 got under way, Reagan's age was often cited. He was sixty-nine. Were he to win the election, he would celebrate his seventieth birthday a few weeks after taking the oath of office.

As one reporter pointed out, William Henry Harrison, the ninth president, was sixty-eight years old when inaugurated. During the inaugural ceremonies, Harrison caught a cold that turned into pneumonia (according to many historians), and he died thirty-two days later.

But Reagan's age never became an important issue in the campaign. This was partly because of his appearance. He was careful about his weight. He did not smoke. He chopped wood, rode horseback (and was often pictured doing so), and swam.

He looked young; he acted young. Indeed, his display of vigor and stamina probably did more to overcome questions about his age than did any other factor.

Reagan made no apologies for his age. He adopted a positive attitude. He sometimes compared himself to Giuseppe Verdi, the Italian opera composer, who wrote the score for *Otello* at the age of seventy-four and for *Falstaff* at eighty, or to Antonius Stradivarius, who made his best violins after he had reached sixty, and was still making them in the year of his death at ninety-two.

Reagan would also joke about his age. After watching himself play the role of George Gipp in a rerun of *Knute Rockne—All American,* he said, "It's like seeing a younger son I never knew I had."

Another time, Reagan cited Thomas Jefferson's advice not to worry about one's age. Then, pausing for effect, he added, "Ever since he told me that, I've stopped worrying."

Reagan held a commanding lead in the polls in the early stages of the campaign. But he committed a series of blunders that caused many voters to have second thoughts about him.

In August, addressing the Veterans of Foreign Wars, Reagan spoke of how the nation had neglected the Vietnam veterans, saying, "We have been shabby in our treatment of those who returned." Then he added, "It is time we recognized that ours, in truth, was a noble cause."

Calling the Vietnam War a "noble cause" raised a storm of protest among those who had opposed the war. It hurt Reagan with the voters.

Not long after, Reagan slipped up again when he proposed that the United States establish an official diplomatic relationship with Taiwan, the Republic of China. Not only was such a move prohibited by the Taiwan Relations Act of 1979, but the very suggestion of it put a strain on relations between the United States and the mainland government the People's Republic of China. In 1978, the United States had recognized the People's Republic as the sole government of China.

Reagan later had to reverse himself, which made him look bad.

In September, Reagan blundered yet again when he

wrongly called Tuscumbia, Alabama, where President Carter had opened his campaign, "the city that gave birth to and is the parent body of the Ku Klux Klan." Reagan knew immediately that to link Carter and the Klan, even vaguely, was a mistake. "I blew it," he said to his advisers.

Within hours, Reagan had to issue an apology to the state of Alabama and the town of Tuscumbia (which was not the birthplace of the Klan). Again Reagan looked bad.

Reagan had never hesitated about giving his opinion on a wide range of topics; it was part of his nature to do so, even on those topics that he did not fully understand. But now, as a candidate for president, his every word was recorded and written down, subjected to close examination, and transmitted to every corner of the world.

When Reagan ran for governor of California the first time, the campaign had been directed by Stuart K. Spencer, who knew politics and politicians as well as anyone. "Where's Stu?" Nancy Reagan began to ask when her husband's campaign began to go awry. "Why isn't Stu here?" Soon after, Spencer was sent for. By the early weeks of September, he was in charge of the candidate. From then on, there were fewer mistakes.

Jimmy Carter was not the most difficult of opponents. A former governor of the state of Georgia, Carter was the first president from the Deep South since before the Civil War. Often described as "good and decent," he represented bright hopes for the nation following the Watergate scandal of the Nixon administration and the blandness of the Ford years.

As president, Carter got high marks for the role he played in the peace negotiations between Israel and Egypt. But this success was forgotten when militant students stormed the American embassy in Teheran, Iran, in November 1979, and took hostage some ninety people, including sixty-six Americans (of whom thirteen were soon released). The students demanded the return of Shah Mohammed Reza Pahlavi for

With former presidents Richard Nixon, Gerald Ford, and Jimmy Carter.

trial. The Shah was undergoing medical treatment in New York City.

To win back the hostages, Carter tried diplomatic pressure and, eventually, a military rescue mission. Neither worked. The hostage ordeal was to plague Carter until the final hours of his administration.

In December 1979, the Soviet Union invaded Afghanistan. Carter reacted by refusing to sell American grain to the Soviets and by calling for a boycott of the Olympic Games which were to be held in Moscow in 1980.

What *really* hurt Carter, though, were economic problems. During the 1950s and 1960s, Americans had enjoyed unprecedented prosperity. They saved and spent more than at any time in history. What had become the American dream—a good job, a home, a car or two, and college for their children—seemed within the grasp of most people.

But during the 1970s, the dream began turning into a nightmare. Inflation was the reason.

Prices went up and up, and showed no signs of declining.

The purchasing power of the dollar plummeted. Poor people and those on fixed incomes suffered the most.

Mild inflation occurs when the price level increases from 2 to 4 percent a year; moderate inflation is about 10 percent a year.

In 1979, the rate of inflation hit 18.2 percent. Many economists feared it might go higher.

At the same time, the nation's economy had all but stopped expanding. Sluggish growth meant that few new jobs were being created. Unemployment was on the rise.

By the end of the decade, interest rates were at near-record levels. Because it was so expensive to borrow money, families were reluctant to purchase homes or cars. Few business people wanted to buy new equipment or improve their plants.

Reagan attacked the Carter administration as the "failed presidency." He charged, "Thanks to the economic policies of the Democratic party, millions of people found themselves out of work."

Reagan also attacked big government, as he had done when running for governor of California. He said that big government was a principal cause of the nation's economic problems. Big government spent too much, and this led to fraud and mismanagement.

What we must have, Reagan said, is "the clarity of vision to see the difference between what is essential and what is merely desirable, and then the courage to bring our government back under control."

Reagan said he had a solution for the nation's economic ills. Opponents called the program Reaganomics.

It called for decreased government spending, a balanced budget, and big cuts in taxes paid by businesses and individuals.

A tax cut, Reagan argued, would stimulate the economy by making available to business people vast sums of money that would otherwise have been taken by the government.

This money would then be invested in business and industry, leading to an expansion of the economy.

The expanded economy would, in turn, provide new jobs and produce an increase in the amount of taxes the government collected. Thus, the money lost by virtue of the tax cut would be replaced by the new taxes produced by the expanding economy.

One other point: While Reagan called for a wholesale reduction in government spending, the one area he believed should not be cut was the military. The Soviet Union, he said, had achieved a dangerous military superiority over the United States. He called, therefore, for a huge increase in defense spending.

Reagan's call for a military buildup came at the right time. Fifty-three Americans had been held hostage in Iran. The Soviet Union, in a savage show of strength, had invaded Afghanistan.

These events upset the American people. According to a poll conducted in 1980 by the University of Chicago's National Opinion Research Council, 60 percent of those surveyed said that too little was being spent on the military. Only 12 percent said that too much was being spent. (Twenty-eight percent thought outlays were about right.) In other words, Reagan's call for increased military spending suited the national mood.

Nancy Reagan did her part during the campaign. She was often seen on television at her husband's side at rallies, receptions, or dinners. On the Reagan campaign plane, she chatted with reporters and passed out chocolates.

Other times, Nancy campaigned on her own. It was hard work and fatiguing, but Nancy always appeared cool, smiling, and smartly dressed. Whenever she campaigned by herself, she made sure she called her husband once or twice a day.

As the campaign headed into its last two weeks, Carter and Reagan stood about even in the polls. On October 28, the Tuesday before the election, the two were to meet in a nationally televised debate. Whoever managed to "win" the debate would probably also win the election.

Reagan had done well in an earlier debate against John B. Anderson, the third-party candidate. But Jimmy Carter, known to be a very skilled debater, was a more threatening opponent.

In preparing for the debate, Reagan practiced by having several of his associates impersonate members of the panel who would be asking the questions, while David Stockman, a young congressman from Michigan, played the role of Carter.

The debate itself covered a wide range of subjects. One topic was nuclear weapons. Carter said, "I had a discussion with my daughter Amy the other day before I came here to ask her what the most important issue was. She said she thought nuclear weapons and the control of nuclear arms."

Carter supporters in the audience gasped at the silliness of their candidate's remark. Amy was twelve years old. For the president to give the impression that he was consulting her about nuclear arms was on a par with Reagan's worst blunders earlier in the campaign.

Reagan made no serious mistakes during the debate. And he scored heavily against his rival during a discussion of Medicare, a government program of hospitalization and medical insurance.

Earlier, Reagan had accused the president of misstating Reagan's stand on certain issues. When Carter attacked his record on Medicare, Reagan felt that Carter was misrepresenting the facts yet another time. He cocked his head, looked at Carter as a father might look at an unruly child, and said, "There you go again."

"There you go again" was the perfect remark for the moment. It diminished Carter in the public's eyes. He never recovered from it.

In his final campaign speech, delivered the day before the election, Reagan asked a series of questions:

"Are you more confident that our economy will create productive work for our society or are you less confident? Do you feel you can keep the job you have or gain a job if you don't have one?

"Are you pleased with the ability of young people to buy a home; of the elderly to live their remaining lives in happiness; of our youngsters to take pride in the world we have built for them?

"Is our nation stronger and more capable of leading the world toward peace and freedom or is it weaker?

"Is there more stability in the world or less?

"Are you convinced that we have earned the respect of the world and our allies, or has America's position across the globe diminished?

"Are you personally more secure in your life? Is your family more secure? Is America safer in the world?

"And most importantly—quite simply—the basic question of our lives: Are you happier today than when Mr. Carter became president of the United States?"

The next day, Reagan swamped Carter and Anderson. He received about 44 million popular votes to about 35 million for Carter and 5.5 million for Anderson. Reagan carried forty-four states for a total of 489 electoral votes. Carter carried only six states and the District of Columbia for a total of 49 electoral votes.

Just sixteen years after he had spoken his mind on Barry Goldwater's behalf, Reagan, the movie actor, the amateur politician, who was approaching his seventieth birthday, had been elected president of the United States.

12

Mr. President

In his inaugural address, delivered on January 20, 1981, Reagan announced the beginning of "an era of national renewal." He said it was time "to reawaken this industrial giant," get government back within its means, and lighten the tax burden.

In foreign affairs, he pledged to "match loyalty for loyalty" with allies and neighbors.

He warned the "enemies of freedom" that "when action is necessary to preserve our national security, we will act . . ."

As Reagan concluded his inaugural address, the revolutionary government in Iran released the fifty-three Americans it had held hostage for 444 days. Reagan sent Jimmy Carter to greet the returning hostages when they arrived in Wiesbaden, West Germany.

Reagan brought with him to Washington a loyal group of Californians to fill the most important jobs on his staff. These included Edwin Meese, who became counselor to the president (and, in 1985, attorney general), and Michael Deaver, deputy chief of staff, who was probably closer to the president than any of his other advisers. (Deaver left the president's staff in 1985 to take a public relations post in Washington.)

Reagan also brought in aides from the outside. James Baker, White House chief of staff (who became secretary of the treasury in 1985) and the man who mapped Reagan's strategy with Congress, was from Texas. Baker had worked for Gerald Ford and George Bush. Indeed, Baker had managed Bush's primary campaign in 1980, and had worked to defeat Reagan. It was rare for a president to pick a close adviser from an "enemy" camp.

Key decisions in the Reagan administration were made by small "working groups" of advisers. The membership of these groups could vary, but usually included Deaver, Baker, or Meese.

Reagan liked to delegate duties and responsibilities. He would appoint someone to accomplish an objective, and then give that individual the authority to attain it. While the president might set basic guidelines, he did not like to get involved in the details of how the goal might be accomplished. He trusted people.

Reagan had been in office only a short time when he declared the nation to be "in the worst economic mess since the Depression." He added, "We are threatened with an economic calamity of tremendous proportions and old business-as-usual treatment can't save it."

Reagan's first act as president was to freeze government hiring. He asked Congress to slash the budget of federal domestic programs. "It's time to try something different," he said to the nation in a televised address early in February 1981.

Monday, the 30th of March 1981, was the seventy-year-old president's seventieth day in office. On his schedule for that day was a luncheon address before 3500 trade union representatives at Washington's Hilton Hotel. While his speech mainly concerned his economic program, he did refer to the nation's social problems, saying, "Violent crime has surged 10 percent, making neighborhood streets unsafe and families fearful in their homes." The union representatives interrupted his speech four times to applaud.

Afterward, his aides at his side, the president walked briskly from the banquet room through a long corridor leading to the doors beyond which the presidential limousine waited. When he came out into the gray afternoon, a reporter asked a question. Reagan, about ready to enter his car, smiled and half-turned toward the man.

Suddenly shots rang out. Later someone would say they sounded like a string of firecrackers. A woman screamed. Reagan froze, looking helpless. Secret Service agent Jerry Parr shoved Reagan into the waiting limousine. The president struck his head on the door frame and went sprawling onto the floor. Then Parr jumped on top of Reagan, trying to protect him with his body. "Take off!" Parr ordered the driver. "Just take off!"

Reagan was in terrible pain. He felt as if someone had stabbed an ice pick in his side. At first, Reagan thought that Parr had broken his ribs when he shoved him into the car. Then the president started coughing up blood. Parr ordered the driver to head for George Washington University Hospital, which was nearby.

Meanwhile, back at the hotel, all was chaos. Sirens screamed as police, Secret Service agents, doctors, and ambulances converged on the scene. A gunman, later identified as twenty-five-year-old John Hinckley, Jr., had fired six shots in two seconds. He wounded four people, including the president. White House Press Secretary James Brady was near death, a bullet in his brain. One of the president's Secret Service agents and a Washington policeman were also victims.

Only quick and expert medical attention saved the president's life. A bullet from Hinckley's gun struck the president's limousine, flattened out into a dime-sized disc, then ricocheted into the president's body. Entering under his left arm, it deflected off a rib and lodged within an inch of his heart. Surgeons opened the president's chest and removed the bullet.

The grace and good humor the president displayed throughout his ordeal helped to reassure the nation that he would recover. He told Nancy Reagan, who rushed to his bedside at the first word of the shooting, "Honey, I just forgot to duck." And when doctors were preparing him for surgery, he remarked to them, "I hope you people are all Republicans."

Reagan was saddened when he learned about the other victims. While the Secret Service agent and the police officer were not seriously wounded, Brady was left partially paralyzed. Hinckley, the gunman, was declared insane at the time of the attempted assassination and was placed in a mental institution.

Reagan remained in George Washington University Hospital for about two weeks. The hospital staff developed a

Well-wishers hang a get-well banner near the hospital where Reagan was treated for gunshot wounds.

deep affection for him. Later in the year, when he was asked by an interviewer what he might have done differently in the first six months of his administration, Reagan grinned and said, "I wouldn't have gone to the Hilton."

As a result of the assassination attempt, security around the president was tightened. Reagan accepted the advice of the Secret Service and began wearing a bulletproof vest in situations that were potentially dangerous.

The attempt on the president's life increased his already sizable popularity. When he went before a joint session of Congress with his economic message on April 28, 1981, he received a thunderous ovation.

His increased popularity helped Reagan to get his economic legislation passed by Congress. In fact, he got pretty much what he asked for, including the biggest tax cut in history.

It was called the Economic Recovery Tax Act of 1981, and it reduced individual and business income taxes by about $33 billion. Congress also passed cuts in the funding for welfare and employment programs, while increasing defense spending.

The Reagan cutbacks represented a significant change in the direction the nation had been heading socially and economically. Indeed, not since the first administration of Franklin D. Roosevelt had there been such an abrupt reordering of the nation's priorities.

Reagan was not prepared for what happened. In mid-1981, the United States fell victim to a major recession. Unemployment soared. Thousands of companies failed. As a result, tax revenues shrank, producing a growing deficit in the federal budget.

To reduce the deficit, Reagan reversed himself and asked Congress for a tax *increase.* In August 1982, Congress passed tax increases totalling about $91 billion. It was the largest tax increase in the nation's history. The economy began to recover in 1983.

Reagan also changed the direction of American foreign policy. Under Presidents Carter, Ford, and Nixon, U.S. policy toward the Soviet Union stressed *détente*—a lessening of tension between nations, sometimes achieved through treaties or trade agreements.

Reagan deemphasized detente. He took a much tougher approach toward the Soviet Union.

This was true even though Reagan kept a campaign promise to American farmers and lifted a ban on the sale of grain to the Soviet Union. Since the embargo served to make more grain available, thus reducing prices, the farmers felt the embargo hurt them as much as it did the Soviets. President Carter had imposed the embargo in response to the Soviet invasion of Afghanistan.

Reagan made no secret of how he felt toward the Soviets. In a mid-1982 commencement address at Eureka College, he reminded his audience of the lack of freedom in the Soviet Union. He accused the Russians of violating treaties, beating down freedom in Poland, and "employing chemical weapons against the freedom fighters of Afghanistan."

In March 1983, while addressing a meeting of Christian evangelists in Florida, Reagan declared that America's conflict with the Soviet Union was a "struggle between right and wrong, good and evil." He called the Soviet Union "an evil empire." "There is sin and evil in the world," he declared, "and we are enjoined by Scripture and the Lord Jesus to oppose it with all our might."

The United States provided the Western European countries of the North Atlantic Treaty Organization (NATO) with a new generation of nuclear missiles—the Pershing 2 and cruise missiles.

Reagan said he was "drawing the line" against Communist interference in Central America. Specifically, the line was drawn in Nicaragua and El Salvador.

Cuba and the Soviet Union supplied war materials to the Sandinista regime in Nicaragua and leftist guerrillas in El

Salvador. The United States, in turn, sent advisers and military equipment to the anti-Sandinista rebels in Nicaragua and the rightest regime in El Salvador.

In October 1983, Reagan ordered the invasion of the Caribbean island of Grenada. More than 6000 U.S. troups, plus 300 soldiers from seven Caribbean countries, took part in the invasion. Its objective: to overthrow a leftist government that had taken control of the island.

U.S. troops captured a huge supply of Soviet-made weapons that had been stockpiled on the island. Reagan charged that Cuba had been planning to use Grenada as a military base.

The Grenada invasion was hailed as a victory by the Reagan administration. About the Middle East there were no such claims, however.

In Lebanon, in fact, Reagan's policies led to tragedy. In June 1982, Israel had invaded Lebanon in an effort to destroy bases of the Palestine Liberation Organization (PLO). The PLO forces had been using the bases to attack settlements in Israel.

Israeli forces quickly smashed PLO strongholds. A cease-fire was then agreed upon and peace talks began. Lebanese and Israeli representatives met to arrange for the withdrawal of all foreign forces from Lebanon.

Reagan sent several U.S. Marine Corps units to Lebanon as part of an international peacekeeping force. The Marines dug in at the airport of Beirut, Lebanon's capital. In October 1983, close to 250 Marines were killed when their Beirut headquarters was bombed in a terrorist attack.

Marine commanders in Beirut were criticized for poor security and their failure to heed warnings that the terrorists would attack. Reagan tried to accept responsibility for the tragedy. He said, "If there is to be blame, it properly rests here in this office and with this president."

The remaining Marines in Lebanon were later withdrawn. So ended a sad chapter in American history.

13

Behind White House Doors

His first weeks in the White House did nothing to change Reagan's easygoing nature and positive attitude. He remarked that the executive mansion, as a combined workplace and residence, reminded him of his early days in Tampico, Illinois. "I'm back living above the store again," he joked.

During an average workday, Reagan allowed himself a less pressured schedule than his predecessors had. Gerald Ford, as president, got up at 5:30 A.M. and began the day with exercises. Jimmy Carter popped out of bed at about the same time.

Lyndon B. Johnson, who occupied the White House for five years beginning in 1963, maintained a killing schedule. His day began at 10:00 A.M. and ran until 4:00 P.M. Johnson then took a two-hour nap, which was followed by work from 6:00 P.M. until midnight.

Reagan, when he became president, had no ambition to try to cram two workdays into one, as Johnson had done. His work habits were well established, and he did not wish to change them. "Show me an executive who works long overtime hours," he once said during the campaign, "and I'll show you a bad executive."

Reagan also had no intention of beginning the day before dawn, as Carter and Ford had. During the campaign, Reagan had once complained to his aide Stuart K. Spencer that his schedule required him to get up too early. "You'd better get used to it, Governor," Spencer replied with a grin. "When you're president, that fellow from the National Security Council will be there to brief you at 7:30 in the morning."

"Well," said Reagan, "he's going to have a helluva long wait."

Reagan wasn't joking. After he became president, the daily national-security briefings were moved to 9:45 A.M.

The White House switchboard had standing orders to call the family living quarters at 8:00 A.M., but the Reagans had usually risen from their king-size bed by that time.

After breakfast with Nancy in the family quarters, Reagan would take the elevator to the first floor. Leaving the elevator, he would greet his Secret Service agents with a cheery "Hi." He would stride down the red carpet toward the Oval Office in the White House's West Office Wing.

During the administration of Theodore Roosevelt, the White House underwent a long-overdue expansion. This included the construction of the West Wing which, for the first time, separated the living spaces from the crowded and sometimes noisy offices and conference rooms. The president's Oval Office was added to the wing in 1909.

Upon arriving at the Oval Office, Reagan would greet his personal secretary. Sometimes he would have a folder of papers to hand her, which he had read or signed the night before.

Reagan would seat himself in his black leather swivel chair behind the massive oak desk. Usually his three top advisers —Edwin Meese, James Baker, and Michael Deaver—would be waiting for him. They would have already had their own breakfasts and taken part in a staff meeting of some twenty Pentagon aides, in which plans for the day and the near future were discussed.

Meese, Baker, and Deaver would sit in front of Reagan's desk or perch on either side of it. The four men would go over the day's schedule (see box), speaking in clipped sentences and exchanging papers.

Reagan's schedule was tight. It took time for him to adjust to that. Not long after he became chief executive, he called himself "a prisoner" of his schedule. "I don't seem to have time to be president," he said.

At 9:45 each morning, the president would listen to a briefing by national-security adviser Robert McFarlane. Others sometimes would join the briefing, including Vice-

Meeting in the Oval Office with top White House aides.

President George Bush, whose advice was highly valued by Reagan. Sensitive international matters would be covered in the national-security briefing.

Next to the Oval Office and separated from it by the office of the president's secretary is the Cabinet Room. It is a light and pleasant room that, like the Oval Office, looks out on the Rose Garden.

Here, the cabinet—the President's board of advisers—meets. The Cabinet Room is also where the National Security Council holds its sessions and where the president talks with legislative leaders or groups that are too large to meet in his own office.

THE SCHEDULE OF
PRESIDENT RONALD REAGAN

January 12, 1984

7:45 A.M.	Working breakfast with Premier Zhao Ziyang of China	Family Dining Room
8:40 A.M.	Signing ceremony with Premier Zhao and departure statements	East Room
9:15 A.M.	Drop by meeting of Small Business Legislative Council	Executive Office Building
9:30 A.M.	Staff time	Oval Office
9:45 A.M.	National-security briefing	Oval Office
10:00 A.M.	Meeting with William Wilson and Archbishop Pio Laghi	Oval Office
10:05 A.M.	Staff time	Oval Office

12:00 noon	Lunch with vice-president and staff time	Oval Office
2:00 P.M.	Meeting with Cabinet Council on Economic Affairs	Cabinet Room
3:00 P.M.	Staff time	Oval Office
4:00 P.M.	Personnel time	Oval Office
4:30 P.M.	Administrative time • Drop by Japanese Trade Mission meeting • Photo with Inspectors General	Roosevelt Room
5:00 P.M.	Taping session • Jesse Owens Award Dinner • Trucking Association Convention • Health Insurance Association • Association of Home Builders • Tribute to Agent Tim McCarthy • Young President's Organization	Diplomatic Reception Room
7:20 P.M.	Depart for performance of *The Hasty Heart*	Kennedy Center

Reagan would often begin Cabinet meetings on a light note. He once told Donald Regan, then Treasury Secretary, that he had discovered after some research that there was a class distinction in the way their very similar Irish names were pronounced. Of the Treasury Secretary's ancestors, the president said, "Those who called themselves 'Ree-gan' were the lawyers and doctors." Of his own forebears, the president said, "It was only the laborers and farmers who called themselves 'Ray-gan.'"

Cabinet meetings would not be packed with excitement. Michael Deaver once remarked in an interview that "some of those Cabinet meetings get a little boring and I doze off."

He added, "I've seen him [the president] when he had difficulty staying awake, but he wasn't the only one in the room that was."

A few days later, Deaver denied that the president had nodded off at Cabinet meetings.

Lunch would usually be at noon in the dining room on the second floor of the White House. Often it would be a "working lunch," with the president playing host to one special group or another. The menu would include a soup course, perhaps filet mignon as a main course, an artichoke salad, California red wine, and a dessert of fruit cooked in syrup. Afterward, the president would return to his desk.

During the day, the president would often drop by various meetings that were being held in other parts of the White House or in the Executive Office Building, the huge nineteenth-century office building that is located just to the west of the executive mansion. He would speak briefly to these groups and his appearance would be taped and photographed.

The president would also meet briefly and informally with other groups who called upon the White House. These get-togethers were usually held in the Diplomatic Reception Room, an oval room on the ground floor, often used as the entrance to the mansion.

During the period that he was governor of California, Reagan's staff would boil down complex issues into one-page memorandums for him to read and act on. When he became president, the memos got longer. Each would conclude with a space for the president to indicate one of four choices:

Approve ____
Approve as Amended ____
Reject ____
No Action ____

The president would not spend long periods agonizing over decisions. He cared little for details.

Those who worked directly for Reagan said he was "undemanding." He rarely put pressure on anyone.

Nancy Reagan, however, was quite the reverse, often concerned about White House matters down to the tiniest detail. She was known to telephone Deaver or Baker several times a day with questions or suggestions about the day's events or Mr. Reagan's schedule.

On Friday afternoons, the president would often summon a helicopter to the White House lawn for the thirty-minute flight to Camp David, the 134-acre presidential retreat in the Catoctin Mountains of Maryland. Camp David offers a swimming pool, bowling alley, tennis courts, bicycle paths, and a theater, as well as a three-hole golf course and a trout stream. There the president and his family could spend the weekend relaxing.

Although they preferred quiet evenings at home, the Reagans enjoyed entertaining. And when they entertained, they did so with glitter and grace.

The Jimmy Carters often kept pomp at a minimum. The Reagans restored it. A color guard returned to precede the guests of honor. Trumpeters on the White House balcony welcomed foreign visitors.

Menus at White House dinners became more elaborate. The guest lists often included a sprinkling of the Reagans' Hollywood chums. These included Frank Sinatra, Jimmy Stewart, Cary Grant, Bob Hope, Charlton Heston, and Audrey Hepburn.

The White House china ordered by Nancy for formal dinners became the subject of a war of words during Reagan's first year in the White House. Made by Lenox, each of the ivory china place settings was edged in red and bore the presidential seal in raised gold lettering. Besides dinner, salad, and bread-and-butter plates and a cup and saucer, each place setting included a fish plate, finger bowl, cereal bowl, bouillon cup, cream-soup cup, demitasse cup, and berry bowl. A total of 220 place settings was purchased. Each setting cost $910.49, for a total of $200,308.

Some people said that Nancy was being extravagant. To offset the criticism, the White House pointed out that it had been fourteen years since china had last been purchased. In addition, the china was paid for by an anonymous donor.

Nancy was also criticized for overspending in redecorating the twenty-five-room upstairs family quarters. The bill amounted to $822,641. However, this money too was raised through private donation.

Nancy chose pink, salmon, and yellow for the family quarters to create rooms that would be bright and cheerful. Curtains and carpeting were replaced. Antique furniture was reupholstered. Many chairs, tables, sofas, lamps, and other possessions with sentimental value were brought from the Reagans' California home.

The president's upstairs study had red carpeting, red-and-white curtains, family photographs, and Western paintings.

In the Yellow Oval Room, where heads of state and other dignitaries met with the president before state dinners, Nancy added yellow sofas and marble-top tables to make the room more comfortable.

For the walls of their bedroom, Nancy chose a hand-painted, salmon-colored Chinese paper. A small table was placed between a salmon-colored sofa and two chairs done in needlepoint. Above their oversize bed, Nancy had hung the painting *Before Moonrise*, by Carroll Sargent Tyson.

Nancy's dressing room was covered with flowered peach paper. A painting of Nancy and daughter Patti hung over a chest of drawers.

Nancy's second-floor office was painted in a soothing green and decorated with prints of wildflowers. Nancy also had an exercise room and a dozen double closets for her clothes.

She brought the stationary bicycle that she used for daily

exercise to the White House. The president had an exercise room added to the White House. During the first year it was available, Reagan added an inch and a half of muscle to his chest doing workouts with a weight machine.

As First Lady, Nancy continued to work on behalf of the Foster Grandparents Program. In this program, older volunteers become friends of orphaned or handicapped children. She had begun working with the organization during the time her husband served as governor of California. She also launched a determined program intended to discourage drug use among young people.

As part of her efforts, the First Lady played herself in an episode of the television situation comedy "Diff'rent Strokes." She was also cohost of the two-hour-long news and information show "Good Morning, America."

Her campaign also involved speech making. Many of her appearances were at schools. A visit to Harshman Junior High School in Indianapolis in 1984 was typical. She received a standing ovation from nearly 1000 students after being welcomed by the student body president.

During her seven-minute address, she told students that drug abuse is "the most pressing problem facing us today. It crosses all lines—social, economic, color, political, geographic—and it's slowly—perhaps not slowly—eating away at our next generation, your generation."

Nancy Reagan said it was "frightening" to talk with second and third graders who said they had been offered drugs.

"The age at which kids start [taking drugs] is getting younger and younger. The same time we are teaching children to read and write, we should be teaching them about drugs," Mrs. Reagan said.

Nancy Reagan was quick to admit that it took time for her to adjust to the role of First Lady. The assassination attempt upon her husband was a setback. "It was sort of a period of shock for longer than I realized," she said.

Reporters often asked her how she would feel should her

Nancy Reagan participating in a discussion about drug and alcohol abuse with students from Little Rock Central High School, Little Rock, Arkansas.

husband decide to run for reelection in 1984. "I will support anything Ronnie wants," was her standard answer.

Despite the comforts of life in the White House and the availability of Camp David, the president missed Rancho del Cielo. Only at the ranch did he feel completely at home. "This is where I restore myself," he told friends he invited there.

To reach the ranch one would drive along a turning, twisting road that wove its way through gullies and steep-sided ravines. Patches of fog rolling in from the sea could cut one's vision. It was a drive that made Nancy nervous.

Trips to the mountain were much easier for the Reagans once he became president. Air Force One, the presidential plane, would land them at nearby Vandenberg Air Force Base, and then a helicopter would take them to the ranch.

From the summit of Bald Mountain, the highest point on Reagan's land, it is possible to look south and get a view of forty miles or so of California coastline. When looking out toward the Pacific, one can see several of the Channel Islands, one of which is Catalina Island, where the Chicago Cubs once trained and where Reagan first visited in 1937 when he served as the team's broadcaster.

When he was at the ranch, Reagan worked. The five-room, almost one-hundred-year-old adobe house depended on two fireplaces for heat, and Reagan took pride in keeping a plentiful supply of firewood handy.

Wearing jeans, leather boots, and a cowboy hat, he often labored to clear trails of brush. Then, using a double-edged ax, he would cut the tree branches into suitable lengths for the fireplaces. The splits were loaded into a cart towed behind a jeep and brought back to the house for stacking.

At Christmas in 1984, the Reagans presented themselves with a bright red, four-wheel-drive pickup truck. The joint gift was for ranch riding and doing chores.

Reagan liked to ride horseback for a couple of hours each morning and to work in the afternoon. His favorite horse, Little Man, was a thoroughbred that Reagan raised from a

At Rancho del Cielo.

colt. Reagan would saddle the horse himself, clean the horse's hooves, and even change his shoes. Reagan had ridden Little Man's mother in one of his movies, *Stallion Road,* and later had bought her and bred her.

The Reagans sometimes went trail riding together. Nancy Reagan, however, was not a relaxed rider. She preferred spending her time at the ranch indoors—reading, planning, and talking on the telephone.

The Reagans raised a few head of cattle on the ranch. They loved dogs. At one time, the dog population included Millie, a black-haired hound; Taca, a female husky; and Victory, a golden retriever. Victory wore a tag marked "1600 Pennsylvania Avenue" (the address of the White House).

Reagan was warm-hearted toward his animals. When a German shepherd named Fuzzy had to be put to sleep because of arthritis in his hips, Reagan had a small ceremony. He fed the dog some treats and said his good-byes. He later buried the dog on a nearby hillside. He scratched the dog's name on a marker and covered the grave with rocks so coyotes would not dig up the body.

A wide assortment of wild animals lived on the property. Deer were everywhere. Bears were sometimes found in the barn. Bobcats and mountain lions would appear suddenly on the roads and trails. When a mountain lion cub was once discovered sleeping in the barn, Reagan wouldn't let anyone disturb it. That night the mother came and took the cub away.

Reagan did little planting on the ranch. He preferred whatever grew naturally. Wildflowers were a special treat. Reagan once took a seed from a pine cone, sprouted it in a coffee can, then planted the seedling not far from the house; now it's a tree.

Reagan's friends sometimes kidded him by saying that he was a frustrated cowboy. Reagan didn't mind. He realized that there was much truth in the jest.

14

Landslide

On October 18, 1983, when Reagan announced officially that he would be a candidate for reelection in 1984, few people were surprised. Even though the first three years of his administration had been marked by tough challenges and strong controversy, Reagan believed in what he was doing and wanted more time to finish the job.

His health was good, his spirits high.

Paul Laxalt, a former governor of Nevada and a close aide of Reagan's, had a simple explanation of why Reagan planned to seek a second term. "He likes the job," Laxalt said.

Again, Reagan chose George Bush to be the vice-presidential candidate.

The Democrats selected Walter F. Mondale as Reagan's opponent. Mondale had served as vice-president from 1977 to 1981 under President Jimmy Carter. Before his election as vice-president, Mondale was a United States senator from Minnesota. He was well known for his liberal views on domestic issues.

Through the first half of 1984, Mondale battled Colorado senator Gary Hart and other Democratic candidates, including the Reverend Jesse Jackson, through one state primary after another. Although Mondale came out of the primary wars with the nomination all but locked up, his candidacy was shaky.

Reagan had no opposition in the primaries. His campaign was also aided by an economy that was beginning to boom. As a result, Reagan was growing stronger week by week.

Some people said that Mondale lacked leadership qualities. It was said that he owed too much to special-interest groups, to women, blacks, and big labor unions. And many people still identified Mondale with the Carter administration and its failures, especially with the hostages taken by the Iranians.

Mondale's campaign needed a lift. It got it in mid-July 1984 when Mondale chose Representative Geraldine A. Ferraro of New York City's borough of Queens to be his vice-presidential running mate. It was a courageous move on Mondale's part. Never before had a major political party chosen a woman to be its vice-presidential candidate.

The Reagan-Bush ticket was still favored to win. But how much of a difference would Geraldine A. Ferraro make? No one knew for sure.

The Mondale campaign got off to a poor start. He began to hear the jeers of pro-Reagan hecklers at every stop. When Mondale attempted to speak in Los Angeles to the students of the University of Southern California, chants of "Mondale's a wimp" almost drowned out what he had to say. He talked about issues in a complicated manner. His speaking style did not excite the voters.

This contrasted with Reagan's optimism, his winning personality, and his ability to appear strong and decisive. Reagan knew how to look like a leader and talk like a leader.

Reagan's campaign stressed that his administration had cut taxes, slowed the rate of the government's growth, slashed inflation and interest rates, and restored the nation's military strength and the respect with which the nation was regarded throughout the world.

One of the most important issues of the campaign was the federal budget deficit. (A deficit results when more money is spent than is collected.) When this happens, the government sells bonds to get the extra money it needs. It later must repay the borrowed money, and pay interest on it as well.

Spending more money than is raised in taxes is standard policy for the government. The nation's wars were financed through deficit spending, as were most public improvements—highways, dams, and canals.

But many economists were getting edgy, saying that Reagan had let the deficit get out of hand. Too big a deficit can lead to a variety of economic ills, inflation being one of them.

Back in 1980, Reagan had promised to cut taxes, raise military spending, and at the same time balance the federal budget—that is, spend no more money than the government took in. At the time, the budget was running a deficit of about $60 billion a year.

Reagan said that his tax-cutting policies would cause such growth in the economy that tax revenues would rise even as tax rates fell. It didn't work out that way. Instead of declining and withering away to nothing, the budget deficit almost tripled, reaching a level of about $175 billion at the time of the 1984 election.

Meanwhile, the national debt (the total amount the federal government owed because of money it had borrowed) had mushroomed in size. By 1985, it was expected to be about $2.5 trillion, two and a half times what it had been when Reagan took office.

Reagan offered the same solution to the problem— economic growth.

Most economists believed a tax increase would be necessary to bring down the budget deficit. Walter F. Mondale announced very early in the campaign that he was in favor of boosting taxes.

Mondale accused Reagan of having no plan to deal with the deficit. Reagan said higher taxes were not the answer. He called Mondale names like "Coach Tax Hike." He said that for the Democrats "every day is April 15" (the day that personal income tax returns are due each year).

As the campaign reached its final stages, Mondale's supporters looked forward to two TV debates with Reagan. They hoped the debates would give their candidate the opportunity to cut into the president's big lead in the national public opinion polls.

The first debate made Mondale's backers very happy. Mondale was confident, even forceful. Reagan, on the other hand, was fumbling and hesitant. The day after the debate, many people said that Reagan's age was the problem, that he had shown all of his seventy-three years.

President Ronald Reagan and Walter Mondale shake hands at the start of the second round of the 1984 presidential debates.

The second debate was televised two weeks later. In it, Reagan had to show that his stumbling performance in the previous debate had been a fluke. He had to show that he was in control. And the public seemed to think he did. Although Mondale scored points, Reagan did nothing to damage his popularity with the American people or his lead in the opinion polls.

On election night, as the results poured in, it was obvious early in the evening that a Reagan landslide was in the making. The television networks showed one state after another falling into the Reagan column. First Reagan won the South, and then the border states. Next, some of the industrial states—Illinois, Ohio, and New York. As early as 8:01 P.M., CBS said that Reagan would be reelected.

In the end, Reagan carried forty-nine states, losing only Walter F. Mondale's home state of Minnesota and the District of Columbia.

Reagan captured 59 percent of the popular vote; Mondale, 41 percent. Reagan's margin of victory in the popular vote was the second highest in history (next to that of Richard M. Nixon over George McGovern in 1972).

Reagan's electoral-vote margin, 525 to 13, was the largest since Franklin D. Roosevelt's in 1936. (Roosevelt had won 523 electoral votes to Alf Landon's 8.)

Mondale won an overwhelming majority of black votes, but Reagan took almost every other category of voter: young, middle-aged, elderly; low-, middle-, and high-income.

Reagan also carried a majority of the women who voted. One of the surprises of the election, according to *The New York Times*, was "the degree to which Representative Geraldine A. Ferraro seemed not to matter."

The Reagans watched the television returns on four sets in a suite at the Century Plaza Hotel in Los Angeles. When his landslide victory became obvious, the president greeted some 3000 cheering, flag-waving supporters in the hotel ballroom. "Four more years . . . four more years," the crowd chanted.

"I think that's just been arranged," Reagan said with a grin.

Then he turned serious and recalled a list of his administration's accomplishments—lower inflation, more jobs, cuts in federal spending, and strengthened military forces.

"But our work isn't finished," he declared. "Tonight is the end of nothing; it is the beginning of everything."

He closed by repeating a slogan that he had used during the campaign: "You ain't seen nothing yet."

15

Second Term

In mid-1986, when the Democratic and Republican parties were preparing to choose the man who would become Ronald Reagan's successor, the *Washington Post* conducted a special survey appraising Reagan's achievements and failures. Most of the praise focused on Reagan's successes in reducing the threat of war with the Soviet Union.

Such praise was justified. In 1981, when Reagan came into office, the Soviet leaders took a hard line. They pressed their supporters in Poland to crush the Solidarity movement. They supported wars of "national liberation" in Cambodia, South Yemen, Ethiopia, Afghanistan, Angola, and Nicaragua. Soviet Marshal Nikolai Ogarhov boasted openly that the Soviet Union would one day surpass the United States in military might.

Reagan responded with a huge military buildup and a proposal for a space-based "shield" that would protect civilian populations from nuclear attack. He called it the Strategic Defense Initiative, or SDI for short.

The Strategic Defense Initiative was to be a multibillion dollar system based mainly in space that would use laser and particle beams to destroy incoming strategic ballistic missiles. Reagan said that the system had the potential to make all offensive nuclear weapons obsolete.

Reagan's opponents nicknamed the Strategic Defense Initiative "Star Wars," after the movie. They said that it would never work. It was "pure fantasy" according to the critics.

One of these critics pointed out that even if SDI did become operational it would have to work perfectly. What good would it do if 90 to 95 percent of all incoming nuclear missiles were shot down? The 5 or 10 percent that managed to get through would be able to inflict enormous destruction and death.

But Reagan paid no attention to the critics. Weapons manufacturers were assigned to begin developing and testing the system.

Yuri Andropov was the leader of the Soviet Union when Reagan first announced SDI. Andropov died in 1984, to be succeeded by Konstantin Chernenko, who died the very next year. Mikhail Gorbachev then became the general secretary of the Communist party of the Soviet Union. As such, he was the nation's leader. Confident and determined, Gorbachev was to transform the Soviet Union with his bold domestic policies.

When Vice-President Bush went to Chernenko's funeral in 1985, he carried an invitation to Gorbachev from President Reagan for a summit conference in the United States. When Gorbachev replied two weeks later, he completed the first of a round of correspondence between the two leaders that was to last for years. In his autobiography, published in 1990, Reagan said that the letters became not only the foundation of a friendship between the two men but also the basis of a better relationship between the two countries.

Early in his second term, Reagan's health became a

national concern. A cancerous tumor was found in Reagan's colon, in the upper part of his large intestine. On July 13, 1985, a team of military and civilian surgeons removed the tumor, along with about two feet of his large intestine. Reagan was to make a complete recovery.

Before the surgery began, Reagan signed documents that temporarily transferred the power of the presidency to Vice-President George Bush. The transfer of authority remained in effect for eight hours.

In November 1985, Reagan and Gorbachev met at a summit conference in Geneva, Switzerland. It marked the first time that the leaders of the United States and the Soviet Union had met in six years. Arms control was to be one of the main topics discussed at the conference. Some of Reagan's advisers suggested that he use SDI as a bargaining chip. Put limits on Star Wars, Reagan was told, and perhaps Gorbachev would agree to cut the Soviet missile force.

But Reagan was quick to veto this suggestion. When it came to SDI, the president would not bend.

President Reagan and Soviet leader Mikhail Gorbachev at their second summit meeting in Reykjavik, Iceland in 1986.

A few days before the Geneva summit was to begin, Gorbachev declared that SDI would be the central issue. He condemned the system, saying it represented a move by the United States to militarize outer space.

Reagan and Gorbachev met for a total of five hours during the two days of meetings at Geneva. While they spoke openly with each other, no major agreements were reached on arms control or on the human-rights issues raised by President Reagan. But the two men agreed that the summit served to ease somewhat the crisis atmosphere between the two nations.

While the Geneva meeting produced little in terms of concrete results, it paid off in one sense for the president. During the 1984 election campaign, polls had shown that many people believed that Reagan's tough-minded stance toward the Soviets could lead the nation into war. After Geneva, however, Reagan started getting the highest marks ever for his handling of foreign policy.

Reagan and Gorbachev held a second summit conference in Reykjavik, Iceland, in October 1986. On the first day of the talks, Gorbachev accepted a U.S. proposal for the elimination of all nuclear missiles based in Europe. The next day, the two leaders discussed eventually eliminating other nuclear weapons as well, including bombers. Reagan believed that the two men might be on the brink of achieving something quite remarkable.

Then, after everything had been decided, Gorbachev said, "This all depends, of course, on your giving up SDI."

Reagan couldn't believe what he had heard. He lost his temper.

Reagan was gruff and unsmiling at the end of the Iceland summit, leading some observers to believe that arms-control talks had broken down completely. But in fact, the two men had agreed on basic terms for what later was to become a historic treaty.

In a third summit conference, held in Washington, D.C., in December 1987, Reagan and Gorbachev signed the

Intermediate Nuclear Force (INF) agreement. It was the first treaty between the superpowers calling for the elimination of an entire class of nuclear weapons. Specifically, it provided for the dismantling of 1,752 American and 859 Soviet missiles with a range of 300 and 3,400 miles. It also provided that inspection teams would be able to visit missile sites to see to it that the treaty was being complied with. Despite the fact that the two men had come to terms on a far-reaching agreement, Reagan admitted after the conference that they were still in dispute over SDI.

The two leaders also made plans to meet a fourth time— in Moscow in May 1988, when Reagan's presidential term would be winding down. It would be Reagan's first trip to the Soviet Union.

It was a journey that Reagan enjoyed. He lunched with Soviet cultural leaders and walked through Moscow's Red Square with Gorbachev. When he and Mrs. Reagan strolled one evening near Spasso House, the U.S. ambassador's residence, where they were staying, they were mobbed by Soviet citizens.

In their meetings, the president and the Soviet leader made progress on an agreement that would reduce long-range nuclear weapons. However, no major agreement was achieved on arms control or on any other issue. Gorbachev, in fact, said that the Moscow summit represented "missed opportunities" on arms control. To Reagan, however, the summit was "a success."

The Moscow summit was more symbolic than anything else. Television and newspapers showed the American and Soviet leaders together, smiling, friendly, open, with the common goal of seeking to reduce tensions between the two countries.

By this time, Gorbachev had begun withdrawing Soviet troops from Afghanistan. He was also encouraging an end to the fighting between U.S.- and Soviet-supported forces in Angola and Cambodia.

Reagan supporters say that he will be remembered as the

president who put an end to military competition between the United States and the Soviet Union, thus ushering out the cold war.

Reagan had second-term foreign policy successes besides those involving Mikhail Gorbachev and the Soviet Union. He saw a peaceful transition in the Philippines from the military dictatorship of Ferdinand Marcos to a democratic government headed by Corazon Aquino.

Terrorism increased throughout the world during the mid-1980s, and Reagan acted decisively to combat it. In October 1985, he ordered a daring midair interception of an Egyptian jet carrying a small group of Palestinian terrorists. The terrorists had hijacked the Italian cruise liner *Achille Lauro* and had killed a wheelchair-bound American passenger before they surrendered to Egyptian authorities. The U.S. aircraft forced the airliner to land in Sicily, where the hijackers were arrested.

In April 1986, two people were killed, including an American serviceman, and some 200 were injured when terrorists bombed a discotheque in West Germany. U.S. officials said that Libyan leader Muammar al-Qaddafi had planned and ordered the bombing.

Reagan, calling the evidence involving Qaddafi "irrefutable," ordered U.S. aircraft based in England to strike targets in the Libyan cities of Tripoli and Benghazi. Qaddafi himself was said to be a target. The attack discouraged the Libyan leader from planning additional terrorist acts against Americans in Europe.

In May 1987, two missiles from an Iraqi warplane hit the *U.S.S. Stark*, an American guided-missile frigate patroling the Persian Gulf. Iraq said that the attack was a mistake. Thirty-seven American crew members died.

Another incident occurred in July 1988, when the *U.S.S. Vincennes*, an American cruiser, shot down an Iranian airliner, mistaking it for a jet fighter. All 290 people aboard were killed. Reagan expressed the nation's deep regret for the loss of life and said that the United States would pay compensation to the families of the victims.

Late in 1988, in his first breakthrough in the Middle East after nearly eight years of trying, Reagan heard Yassir Arafat, chairman of the Palestine Liberation Organization (PLO), renounce terrorism and proclaim Israel's right to exist. Reagan then ordered direct talks with the PLO.

Reagan credited his foreign policy successes to the build-up of American military forces, plus his willingness to be both patient and firm.

That strategy, however, did not work in Nicaragua, where Congress forced him to seek a diplomatic solution. Reagan would have preferred to keep supporting the "contra" rebels in their efforts to overthrow the Sandinista government. Nor did Reagan's policies have much effect in South Africa, which resisted U.S. pressure to abolish apartheid, the government's official policy of racial segregation.

Reagan's policy also failed in Lebanon, where seven Americans continued to be held as hostages. This deeply pained the president. When he was presented with what he thought was a chance to win the release of the hostages, he jumped at it. In doing so, he triggered what was to become the worst scandal of his administration, known as the "Iran-contra" affair.

The scandal began when officials of the government of Israel approached high-ranking officials of the Reagan administration with a secret plan to sell missiles and spare parts for weapons to politically moderate elements in Iran. The Israelis said that the sale would be helpful in gaining the release of the Americans who were being held hostage in Lebanon.

The Reagan administration had always said that it would never deal with terrorists. It would be foolish even to consider doing so. In addition, the 1979 Arms Export Control Act had banned arms sales to Iran. Nevertheless, Reagan authorized the sale.

That was not the worst of it. Apparently unknown to

Reagan, the money paid by the Iranians was to go to rebel forces—the contras—fighting in Nicaragua. The contras, strongly supported by members of the president's National Security Council, were fighting against the Communist-supported Sandinista government. However, the U.S. Congress had voted to halt all financial aid to the contras.

Reagan ordered an investigating committee, headed by former Texas senator John Tower, to look into the Iran-contra mess. The result was a 300-page report issued early in 1987 that depicted the president as confused and uninformed. It declared that his personal management style had prevented Reagan from having control over those who worked for him.

The Tower Commission put "primary responsibility for the chaos" caused by Iran-contra on Donald T. Regan, the White House chief of staff. The report said that Regan had given the president bad advice and had failed to grasp the serious legal and political problems involved.

Televised hearings before Senate and House committees began early in May 1987 and lasted until August. Tales were told of a "shredding party" in which potential evidence was destroyed, of cash handed over to contra leaders outside the White House gates, and of Iranians being given a late night tour of the White House.

The revelations sent out shock waves that rocked the Reagan presidency. It reminded people of Watergate. There were even rumors that Reagan himself might be forced to resign. His popularity took a nosedive.

Reagan did not do much to help himself. He responded to the charges with statements that sometimes raised as many questions as they answered. Not long after the public hearings got under way, Reagan told a group of reporters: "I'm hopeful that I'm finally going to hear some of the things I'm still waiting to hear about."

"Don't you know what you did?" a reporter asked.

"I know what I did, and I have told all of you repeatedly

what I did, and now I'm going to quit talking to you and go into the office," he replied, scowling.

It was not a happy time in the White House. The president's energy and enthusiasm were drained even more by the fact that, according to some polls, more than half of the public believed he was lying.

"Does the president feel bad? No doubt about it," said Senator Charles E. Grassley of Iowa. "He feels ill-treated. He's a sensitive man. Emotionally, he's been hurt."

Late in 1987, when the congressional committees that had investigated the Iran-contra affair issued their joint report, Reagan was strongly criticized. A majority of the committee members said that he was chiefly responsible for the wrongdoing by his aides and that he had failed to meet the constitutional obligation to "take care that the laws are faithfully enforced."

Marine Lieutenant Colonel Oliver North being sworn in prior to testifying before the House and Senate Iran-contra committee in 1987.

Marine Lieutenant Colonel Oliver L. North, a National Security Council aide, was the person who directed much of the undercover operation. In 1989, a jury in federal district court in Washington, D.C., convicted North of interfering with Congress's investigation of the affair. North was also found guilty of destroying documents important to the investigation and of helping to produce a false timetable of Iran-contra events.

In 1988, his final year in office, President Reagan managed to put Iran-contra behind him and to bounce back. He recovered his physical health and got a political and emotional boost from his summit meeting with Mikhail Gorbachev in December 1987. His popularity index started climbing again.

The Reagans began planning the lives they would lead after January 20, 1989, the day that Reagan's successor would take the oath of office. Mr. and Mrs. Reagan would be living in Bel Air, California, a wealthy community near Los Angeles. There, a group of Reagan's friends paid $2.5 million for a home for him and Nancy Reagan.

During the summer and fall of 1988, Reagan was also energized by the presidential election campaign, in which George Bush faced Michael Dukakis, governor of Massachusetts. At the Republican national convention in New Orleans, Bush's supporters presented the vice-president as the heir to President Reagan. The Republicans reminded voters of the successes of the Reagan years and of their deep affection for Mr. Reagan himself.

After Reagan had addressed the convention, receiving one loud burst of cheers and applause after another, and he and Mrs. Reagan were preparing to leave New Orleans, George Bush went with them to the airport. The vice-president followed the president to the steps of Air Force One and then leaned forward to whisper the name of Dan Quayle in the president's ear. Bush planned to select Quayle to be his vice-president, but at the time, the choice was still a secret.

Reagan campaigned hard for the Bush-Quayle ticket, traveling to Texas, California, Michigan, Illinois, and Indiana. People lined roadways and stood in front yards and parking lots, hoping to catch a glimpse of the president as the presidential caravan whisked by.

At each stop, Reagan was warm and friendly. He thanked the bands that greeted him, mentioned the names of local candidates, and praised George Bush. All speeches ended with the same line: "So I ask you just one last time, on Election Day, will you go out and win one for the Gipper?"

Reagan could not help but be cheered by George Bush's decisive election victory. During the campaign, neither Bush nor Dukakis presented the voters with any big issues to consider. A vote for Bush was seen as a vote to continue the peace and prosperity of the Reagan years. It was, in a sense, an endorsement of Reagan and his policies.

It is rare in American politics when voters elect a man handpicked by the incumbent to succeed him. Not since 1877, when Republican Ulysses S. Grant was followed in office by Rutherford B. Hayes, had a president retired after two full terms and been succeeded through election by someone from the same party.

It was also noted that Reagan was the first president to turn the White House over to his vice-president since 1837, the year Democrat Andrew Jackson was followed by Martin Van Buren.

Reagan took his departure from the White House in stride. "He is totally comfortable with the fact of leaving and more relaxed about it every day," said White House spokesperson Marlin Fitzwater (who was to stay on to serve in the same role for Bush). "He's very satisfied that he has done everything he could do."

16

Reagan's Critics

Arctic cold withered snowblown Washington on the weekend of President Reagan's second inaugural. When the temperature plummeted to nine degrees and threatened to go lower, Reagan, acting on the advice of the Inaugural Committee, decided to cancel the inaugural parade and outdoor oath-taking ceremony. The latter was moved indoors to the Capitol rotunda.

The bitter cold, however, did not stop the Reverend Jesse Jackson and about 1000 of his supporters from staging a protest march and rally on Saturday afternoon of the inauguration weekend.

The march was led by nearly a dozen disabled and handicapped persons who propelled themselves forward on crutches and in wheelchairs. Jackson, who wore a sign that read JOBS NOT BOMBS, was in the first row of marchers. Linking arms with him were John E. Jacobs, president and chief executive officer of the National Urban League, Mayor Richard Hatcher of Gary, Indiana, and former U.S. assistant attorney general Roger Wilkins and other black leaders.

As the marchers filed down Pennsylvania Avenue past the White House in the subfreezing temperatures, they chanted slogans condemning Reagan's budget cuts and U.S. policies in Central America and South Africa.

At the rally, Jackson denounced a wide range of Reagan's policies. In an address that was similar to those he delivered during the presidential campaign, Jackson charged that "the rich have gotten richer and the poor have gotten poorer" under Reagan. He said that the president and his policies were examples of "Robin Hood in reverse."

Loud criticism of Reagan's policies had begun to be heard in 1982 and 1983. Jesse Jackson and other black leaders represented only one group of his critics. Women and environmentalists were two others.

Those representing minority groups complained bitterly about Reagan's insensitivity to those in need. They cited cuts in food stamps, unemployment compensation, housing subsidies, urban mass transit, student loans, child nutrition programs, and aid to families with dependent children.

John E. Jacobs of the National Urban League summarized the views of many black leaders when he said, "President Reagan has demonstrated insensitivity to the problem of poverty. His administration cut back on civil-rights enforcement, cut back on survival programs, cut back on human investments such as education and job training. These policies significantly hurt blacks, whose unemployment and poverty rates rose sharply."

Jacobs also criticized the Reagan administration for "its refusal to appoint more than a token number of blacks to high positions. . . ."

Benjamin Hooks, the head of the National Association for the Advancement of Colored People (NAACP), saw the president's policies as bringing new "hardship, havoc, despair, pain, and suffering on blacks and other minorities."

Reagan, naturally, did not agree with such criticism. He believed that black Americans would be able to reap greater benefits from his programs than from the traditional system of government supports. Speaking to delegates of the annual convention of the NAACP in July 1981, Reagan declared: "Many in Washington over the years have been more dedicated to making people government-dependent, rather than independent. They've created a new kind of bondage. Just as the Emancipation Proclamation freed black people 188 years ago, today we need to declare an economic emancipation."

This would come about, Reagan predicted, through his recovery program, which would lift the "entire country and not parts of it."

This is what Reagan believed. The *Los Angeles Times,* in quoting one of Reagan's aides, once said: "His is a philosophy of self-reliance. He believes the more you depend on government, the greater the narcotic effect it has on you."

There was no indication that Reagan's beliefs won him any support among blacks. Indeed, in the presidential election of 1984, fewer than 10 percent of blacks cast their votes for Reagan.

Women were also said to lag in their support of Reagan and his policies. Before the election of 1984, there was much discussion of how women voters were much less inclined than men to cast their ballots for Reagan. This situation had created what was called a *gender gap.*

A *New York Times*/CBS News poll that was taken in mid-1983 revealed that among Republicans the difference between men's approval of Reagan and women's was a startling 21 percentage points.

Why was there a gender gap? And why was it so wide? There are several reasons.

Reagan would not support the passage of the Equal Rights Amendment. He angered working women when he suggested that part of the nation's unemployment problem resulted from an increase of women in the work force.

Reagan enraged feminist organizations by his long-term

support for those who were seeking to make abortion illegal. "Abortion either is the taking of human life or it isn't," Reagan said. "And if it is—and medical technology is increasingly showing it is—it must be stopped."

Representative Olympia Snow of Maine saw Reagan's gender gap as a generation gap. "He's just not capable of understanding the problems of today's women," she declared.

Women's organizations said the president did not name enough women to important posts. Reagan, however, was the first president to appoint a woman to serve on the Supreme Court. During July 1981, he chose Sandra Day O'Connor to fill a Court vacancy.

In addition, Reagan was the first president to have three women serving in Cabinet-level positions at the same time. The women were Margaret M. Heckler, secretary of health and human services; Elizabeth H. Dole, secretary of transportation; and Jeane J. Kirkpatrick, U.S. ambassador to the United Nations.

With Pope John Paul II in Rome in 1982.

Nancy Reagan came in for her share of criticism, too. American women of the 1980s did not always see eye-to-eye with her. Many considered her too "wifely." "She is constantly echoing her husband," said Gloria Steinem, editor of *Ms.* magazine and a leader in the women's movement. "How can two people really be so constantly adoring of each other?" Betty Friedan, another noted feminist, chided Nancy Reagan because "she has not advanced the cause of women at all."

In early 1991, an unauthorized biography of Nancy Reagan stirred much discussion because of its highly unflattering portrait of the former First Lady. Nancy Reagan was depicted as power hungry and manipulative.

Almost from the day Reagan appointed him to be secretary of the interior, James Watt made conservation and wildlife groups unhappy, and that is putting it mildly. From Wyoming, with a law degree from the University of Wyoming, the forty-three-year-old Watt made abrupt changes in Department of Interior policy.

Previous administrations, both Democrat and Republican, had championed environmental preservation for the federal government's enormous land holdings. But Watt sought to make these lands available for commercial development. He said, "We will mine more, drill more, cut more timber to use our resources rather than simply keeping them locked up."

Watt offered a billion acres of offshore lands to oil company drillers. This was more than ten times the amount of offshore acreage proposed for oil exploration and leasing in the entire history of the United States.

Watt also proposed that by the turn of the century the remaining 80 million acres of U.S. wilderness be made available for drilling and mining.

Although many people were in favor of the commercial development of public lands, Watt wanted to go too far too fast. His proposals stirred a hornet's nest of protest.

Reagan did not pay much attention to what Watt was doing, at least at first. He was occupied with his economic program and other matters he felt to be more important.

It has also been said that Reagan is not much of an expert on the environment. He once erroneously claimed, for example, that Mount St. Helens, the western Washington volcano that became active during the early 1980s, spewed more sulfur dioxide into the atmosphere than did American automobiles.

Reagan tried to take some of the heat out of the Watt controversy with humor. He told a joke about an environmentalist who found a sure way to make his children behave. "He scared them into being good," Reagan said, "by telling them that James Watt would get them."

The humor didn't work. Watt's policies and blunt manner in pursuing them eventually led to his downfall. By late 1983, calls for his resignation were coming from Republicans as well as Democrats. The pressure forced Watt to resign. Reagan named William P. Clark to succeed him.

America changed during the 1980s, but Reagan seemed not to notice. A growing American underclass was one such change. The underclass is characterized by high youth unemployment and school dropout rates, by illiteracy and crime, by homelessness and drug abuse. The social policies of the Reagan administration turned a blind eye toward these problems.

"The last Reagan budget calls for increased spending for the Pentagon, while shaving—at least in terms of real dollars—spending for child nutrition programs that have been shown to make a difference in the ability of poor children to learn," said Dorothy Gaiter, writing in the *Miami Herald*. "Financial-aid programs for poor young people who need them to go to college also have been cut."

Asked Ms. Gaiter: "How will this nation compete with Japan and other producer nations if its population . . . lacks the education and training for the new technological age?

"Isn't this a national security issue? Where will our national pride be then?"

A survey conducted by the *Washington Post* in mid-1988

showed that most people believed that Reagan cared more about the interests of the wealthy than about those of the average citizen. Three out of five people agreed with the statement that Reagan was a rich man's president. Slightly over half said that he was unfair to the poor, and nearly half said that he was unfair to the middle class.

"He should have been more interested in the individuals that needed help," said one woman who was polled. "He was much too interested in big business."

Reagan proposed policies that were wrongheaded, no doubt about it. He also made some bad appointments.

But the criticism that followed a Reagan goof never seemed to put too much of a dent in his popularity. Although his popularity tottered after the Iran-contra affair, the public eventually forgave him, and his approval rating went up again.

Reagan was, in fact, sometimes referred to as the "Teflon president." Like a stick-resistant frying pan, he seemed to have some magic shield that prevented criticism from adhering to him. This was true, at least in part, because of his personality—his good cheer, his sense of "can-do" optimism, and his obvious enjoyment of his job.

In 1985 President Reagan was operated on for removal of a cancerous tumor in his colon. Here, he and Mrs. Reagan wave to well-wishers outside Bethesda Naval Hospital.

17

Reagan and History

How will Ronald Reagan look to historians? What is going to be said and written of him fifty or one hundred years from now?

The truth is that presidents do not have a great deal of control over how history comes to regard them. Their reputations usually depend more on events that occur after they leave office than on what they feel they have accomplished.

When Reagan took office in 1981, he made it clear that he did not intend to lead the nation down the road it had been traveling. He said he was going to change things. And he did. He reduced taxes. He cut the rate of growth of federal spending. He strengthened the military.

Some people said that the changes Reagan triggered were misguided, even tragic. They said that Reagan undermined social gains that had been accepted for half a century.

Reagan paid no heed to his critics. As he got set to begin his second term, he planned to "stay the course." He would continue to give priority to defense spending over social needs. He would not call for new taxes to solve the problem of the growing budget deficit.

Reagan was successful in putting an end to inflation and in reducing the unemployment rate. Tax cuts he called for helped to stimulate the economy. During Reagan's two terms, the nation enjoyed the longest period of peacetime prosperity ever.

But many economists believe that Reagan's policies did grave damage to the nation's financial health. Deep tax cuts combined with a huge increase in military spending resulted in enormous budget deficits.

In Reagan's final year in office, the national debt stood at $2 trillion, almost half of it accumulated during the Reagan years. Two trillion dollars amounts to about $30,000 for every American family. At the time, about 40 percent of all income tax dollars were going, not to reduce the debt, but merely to pay interest on it.

Economists say that the debt will weigh heavily on the nation's economy for years to come. Mark Green, president of the Democracy Project, a public policy institute, called the debt, ". . . a ball and chain around the neck of economic growth."

Economists are fearful that the debt burden will cause interest rates to remain unusually high and will make it difficult for American industries to compete with foreign companies. The huge debt will also restrict the government's ability to help the unemployed, the homeless, and the poor.

Senator Daniel P. Moynihan of New York, quoted in *The New York Times* in 1986, called Reagan an "immensely popular" president. "We need a popular president," said Moynihan. "The social order is peaceable and in good order.

"But," Moynihan added, "he has crippled the economy of the nation and this will be with us for the rest of the century."

Historians are likely to treat President Reagan more kindly when it comes to foreign policy matters. He supported freedom fighters in Afghanistan, Angola, and Nicaragua. He

fought terrorists with deeds as well as with words. He proposed and stayed with SDI and signed the first arms-reduction agreement with the Soviet Union.

At the end of 1988, Mikhail Gorbachev appeared before the United Nations to propose making sizable cuts in Soviet military forces. He was, in effect, suggesting an end to the cold war.

Reagan, as president, saw Gorbachev a final time in December 1988, less than seven weeks before he was to leave the White House. It was during the time Gorbachev was in New York City to speak before the United Nations.

Reagan, George Bush, who had been elected president just a few weeks before, and Gorbachev met on Governors Island in New York Harbor. Reagan was encouraged by how well Bush and Gorbachev got along together. It made Reagan feel optimistic about the future.

Unlike some of the presidents immediately preceding him, namely, Jimmy Carter, Richard Nixon, and Lyndon Johnson, Ronald Reagan left the White House with his popularity intact. In retirement, he appeared in public only

President Reagan celebrated his eightieth birthday in 1991.

rarely. He seldom had any comment to make on the issues that occupied him during his eight years in office.

He kept busy writing his autobiography, which was released in 1990. Titled *An American Life*, it recounts his years in the Oval Office.

The book, however, sheds no light on the Iran-contra affair, revealing even less than news stories that appeared at the time. Reagan insists that he did not trade arms for hostages (although he admits it looks that way).

In the book, Reagan said that one of his regrets as president was never being able to take Mikhail Gorbachev on a helicopter trip across the United States to show him how Americans lived. "From the air I would have pointed out an ordinary factory and showed him its parking lot filled with workers' cars," Reagan said. "Then we'd fly over a residential neighborhood and I'd tell him that's where those workers lived—in homes with lawns and backyards. . . ."

Reagan said that he even dreamed of landing in one of those neighborhoods and inviting Gorbachev to walk down a street with him. Reagan imagined then saying to Gorbachev, "Pick any home you want; we'll knock on the door and you can ask the people how they live and what they think of the system."

Throughout the Reagan presidency, Americans enjoyed world peace and unprecedented prosperity. The significance of what he accomplished may fade with the passage of time. But at the time he returned to private life, most Americans agreed that the country was better off because of the Reagan presidency. And most believed that history would deliver a kindly judgment of his efforts.

Important Dates in
Ronald Reagan's Life

1911   Born February 6 in Tampico, Illinois

1932   Graduated from Eureka College

1937   Made film debut in *Love Is on the Air*

1940   Married Jane Wyman

1941   Birth of daughter, Maureen Elizabeth

1942–1945   Served in U.S. Army Air Corps

1945   Adopted son, Michael Edward

1947–1952; 1959, 1960   President, Screen Actors Guild

1949   Divorced from Jane Wyman

1949–1950   Chairman, Motion Picture Industry Council

1952   Married Nancy Davis

1952   Birth of daughter, Patricia Ann (Patti)

1954–1962   Host of a weekly television series, "The GE Theater"

1958   Birth of son, Ronald Prescott (Ron)

1962–1965   Host of a weekly television series, "Death Valley Days"

1966   Elected governor of California

1970   Reelected governor of California

1980   Elected president of the United States

1981   Shot in an assassination attempt

1983   U.S. forces invade the Caribbean island of Grenada

1984   Reelected president of the United States

1985   Met with Soviet leader Mikhail Gorbachev in Geneva, Switzerland

1986   Explosion of space shuttle *Challenger* and death of its seven crew members

1986   Ordered U.S. war planes to bomb targets in Tripoli and Benghazi, Libya

1986   Met with Soviet leader Mikhail Gorbachev in Reykjavik, Iceland

1987   Submitted nation's first trillion dollar budget ($1,024,300,000,000) to Congress

1987   Stock market crashes with Dow Jones industrial average plummeting 508 points

1987   Met with Soviet leader Mikhail Gorbachev in Washington, D.C.; signed the Intermediate Nuclear Forces (INF) Treaty

1988   Met with Soviet leader Mikhail Gorbachev in Moscow

1991   Celebrated his eightieth birthday

Futher Reading

Blumenthal, Sidney and Thomas Byrne Edsall, eds. *The Reagan Legacy.* New York: Pantheon Books, 1988.

Boyarsky, Bill. *The Rise of Ronald Reagan.* New York: Random House, 1968.

Cannon, Lou. *President Reagan: The Role of a Lifetime.* New York: Simon & Schuster, 1991.

Deaver, Michael K. and Mickey Herskowitz. *Behind the Scenes: In Which the Author Talks about Ronald and Nancy Reagan and Himself.* New York: William Morrow & Co., 1988.

Edwards, Anne. *Early Reagan: The Rise to Power.* New York: William Morrow & Co., 1987.

Evans, Rowland and Robert Novak. *The Reagan Revolution.* New York: E. P. Dutton, 1980.

Johnson, Haynes. *Sleepwalking Through History: America in the Reagan Years.* New York: W. W. Norton, 1991.

Kelley, Kitty. *Nancy Reagan: The Unauthorized Biography.* New York: Simon & Schuster, 1991.

Lawson, Don. *The Picture Life of Ronald Reagan.* New York: Franklin Watts, 1985.

Leamer, Laurence. *Make Believe: The Story of Nancy and Ronald Reagan.* New York: Dell Publishing Co., 1983.

Lewis, Joseph. *What Makes Reagan Run.* New York: McGraw-Hill Book Co., 1968.

Reagan, Maureen and Dorothy Herrmann. *First Father, First Daughter: A Memoir.* Boston: Little, Brown & Co., 1989.

Reagan, Michael with Joe Hyams. *On the Outside Looking In.* New York: Zebra Books, 1988.

Reagan, Nancy and Bill Libby. *Nancy.* New York: William Morrow & Co., 1980.

Reagan, Nancy and William Novak. *My Turn: The Memoirs of Nancy Reagan.* New York: Random House, 1989.

Reagan, Ronald. *An American Life.* New York: Simon & Schuster, 1990.

Reagan, Ronald with Richard Hubler. *Where's the Rest of Me?* New York: Duell, Sloan, Pearce, 1965.

Regan, Don. *For the Record.* San Diego, Calif.: Harcourt, Brace, Jovanovich, 1988.

Schieffer, Bob and Gary Paul Gates. *The Acting President.* New York: E. P. Dutton, 1989.

Speakes, Larry and Robert Pack. *Speaking Out: The Reagan Presidency from Inside the White House.* New York: Charles Scribners, Sons, 1988.

Stockman, David A. *The Triumph of Politics: The Inside Story of the Reagan Revolution.* New York: Avon Books, 1987.

Thomas, Tony. *The Films of Ronald Reagan.* Secaucus, N. J.: Citadel Press, 1980.

Index

Index

About the Author

George Sullivan is a well-known author of books for children and young adults, with more than one hundred titles to his credit. Before becoming a full-time author in the mid-1960s, Mr. Sullivan worked in public relations and in publishing. Before that, he served in the Navy as a journalist. He grew up in Springfield, Massachusetts, and graduated from Fordham University in New York City.

His many interests are reflected in his writings. Subjects of his popular biographies for young readers have included President George Bush, Pope John Paul II, Egyptian president Anwar Sadat, Soviet leader Mikhail Gorbachev, boxing champion Muhammad Ali, Olympic gold-medal gymnasts Mary Lou Retton and Nadia Comaneci, and baseball star Reggie Jackson.

Photo Acknowledgments   AP/Wide World Photos: pages 8, 13, 45, 49, 89, 73, 77, 108, 132; Herman Darvick Collections: pages 42, 43; Eureka College: page 22; Michael Evans/The White House: pages 81, 95; Mary Anne Fackelman/The White House: page 102; Jack Kightlinger/The White House: pages 103, 125; Palmer Communications, Inc.: page 28; Reuters/Bettmann: page 113; Karl Schumacher/The White House: page 66; Pete Souza/ The White House: page 131; UPI/Bettmann: pages 119, 128.